D0122084

Origins of the Universe
and What It All Means

Origins of the Universe and What It All Means

Carole
Firstman

DZANC
BOOKS

DZANC BOOKS

5220 Dexter Ann Arbor Rd.
Ann Arbor, MI 48103
www.dzancbooks.org

Parts of this book have been published, in varying forms, in *Colorado Review, Knee-Jerk Magazine, Lifestyle Magazine, Man in the Moon: Essays on Fathers and Fatherhood, Reed Magazine, South Dakota Review,* and *Watershed Review.*

First US edition: August 2016

ISBN: 978-1-938103-91-9

Book design by Steven Seighman

Library of Congress Cataloging-in-Publication Data

Names: Firstman, Carole, 1964- author.
Title: Origins of the universe and what it all means : a memoir / Carole Firstman.
Description: Ann Arbor, MI : Dzanc Books, [2016]
Identifiers: LCCN 2015035099 | ISBN 9781938103919
Subjects: LCSH: Firstman, Carole, 1964—Family. | Authors, American—
   21st century—Family relationships. | Fathers and daughters—United
   States. | Essayists—United States—Biography. | Authors, American—
   21st century—Biography.
Classification: LCC CT275.F5547 A3 2016 | DDC 808.84—dc23LC record
   available at http://lccn.loc.gov/2015035099

Printed in the United States of America

10   9   8   7   6   5   4   3   2   1

To my family of origin: Bruce, Aranga, and David.
And to Karl, the center of my universe.

Contents

PART I

Light, Time, Earth

One

In the beginning there was darkness.

Two

Watch us.

We barreled across the desert toward Death Valley, gray waves of heat seething from the highway. The top of the Karmann Ghia was off and my mother's brown hair flew wildly around her sweating face. It was nearly noon. The sun blazed directly overhead. It must have been a hundred and five degrees by then. The engine ran hot and if we didn't get there soon we'd overheat. Stranded on the road.

Me in the backseat: sitting squarely in the middle, my legs folded, sticky against white vinyl. I was five years old. My sweater wrapped around my forehead like a turban, tight; the empty arms streamed behind in the wind, flapping between my shoulder blades. I pretended the sweater sleeves were my hair. Long, luxurious. Sexy. Yes, sexy—even at five, I knew what that meant. I'd seen plenty of pictures, glossy pages my father had thumbtacked to the wall at home, a mosaic of *Playboy* centerfolds next to his desk, all of them honey-skinned with waist-long hair draped between their breasts. My favorite was a Polynesian-looking woman with thick wooden bracelets and a tie-dye scarf knotted above one ear. One time I stripped down to my blousy cotton under-pants and wore the necklace I'd found at the back my father's bottom desk drawer—a peace sign pendant on a long, heavy gold chain, which I now assume a certain student had given him as a gift—and veiled my short, pixie-cut hair in a tablecloth. Alone in my parents' bedroom I drew the tablecloth tightly around the top of my head and held it in place above one ear, like the woman in the photo. I paraded in front of the full-length mirror, stepping diagonally to one side, spinning abruptly on my heels in order to catch the chain's reflection as it bounced against my skin. The tablecloth billowed from my shoulders then draped toward the center of my chest, framing the pendent that dangled just above my navel. Two more steps and turn again. Billow, sparkle, drape. Back and forth I went in front of the mirror, pivoting so quickly I almost lost my balance.

In the car, I imagined myself again as that Polynesian woman. I bounced with the road beneath us, beneath the tires, tires that smelled like tar in that heat. Up ahead, the asphalt ribboned up and down like a gentle rollercoaster. I held my breath every few seconds, just for an instant each time; it helped me hold onto the falling feeling in my stomach. Falling with each decline. *Yes. Now again.* "Faster," I yelled, or maybe I just thought it. *Faster.*

That summer, my mother was twenty-four, a grad student studying plant pathology. My father was forty-one, a professor at Cal Poly Pomona. His mission to collect spiders, specimens for his class on the evolution of arachnids, meant a working getaway weekend for him, for us. Underneath the passenger seat, a shoe-box rattled with empty jars and half-filled bottles of formaldehyde. Several times that day, and throughout the weekend, my father pulled over when he got the whim. He'd traipse through the gravel on his hands and knees. My mother carried the box of jars while he peered between rocks. He captured scorpions, tarantulas, and desert weevil beetles with an overturned glass jar and three-by-five index cards covered with obsolete to-do lists or random notes-to-self: "Milk, cottage cheese, bread," "arterial system: peri-intestinal vascular membrane." Recently, while cleaning out my father's home, I found a box of letters and a tattered card on which was scratched, "Fondly, P." There in the desert, with one swift move, he would flip the jar and the card, drop the live spider into another jar filled with formaldehyde, then screw on a lid to seal it tight. Death was instant. Then back to the car.

Behind the wheel, my father stepped on the accelerator. He turned the radio dial. The Mamas and the Papas' "California Dreamin'" blared from the dashboard, the words swept up by scarves of heat and spewed over the cactus-spotted sand.

As an adult, the memories click for me like a slideshow, each landscape a framed portrait. Isolated. Self-contained. Cropped. I recall a certain spot on the road to Furnace Creek, somewhere in the middle of that expansive desert. The Kodachrome slide in my mind features a straight segment of highway, one lane in each direction divided by a double yellow line. Black asphalt shoots diagonally across the frame from bottom right to top left, leading the eye from a textured foreground to a blurry, westbound destination. Alongside the road is a diamond-shaped sign with an arrow pointing to the right. It seems contradictory—a warning for an upcoming right turn on what appears to be a straight stretch of road. Surely it's just my memory that's cropped the actual curve in the road from the snapshot frame. Surely my parents saw the road and the curve, too.

High noon: through the wind my mother silently argued with my father, her lips pinched, her eyes narrowed to slits.

My father didn't curse or raise his voice. He just stated the facts. "Her name is Pat," he said. "She needs a pad, a place to crash. Just for a while. A few weeks."

My mother stared out the windshield. The back of her neck splotched red. Heat rash, perhaps.

"No reason to get bent out of shape," my father said. "If you want to keep living with me, and I want you to, the house is plenty big. Pat can live downstairs. Otherwise, you're free to go."

My mother still said nothing, just turned her head to the right. Her eyes trained on a yucca plant rooted in the roadside gravel. Its pointy leaves barbed dangerously close to our car. We zoomed past, the white bloom arching, swaying overhead. Swaying above my shirtsleeve hair.

Three

I recently found a scorpion on my father's desk, which I have since stolen. Not a live creature, but a specimen, long pickled in formaldehyde. The handwritten label inside the jar reads: *Paruroctonus silvestrii: Las Estacas, Mexico—1971.* The scorpion floats in suspended animation, trapped in the jar I balance on the flat of my palm, its body preserved for display. Appearing neither dead nor alive, it hovers near the bottom, leaving an almost imperceptible gap between its abdomen and the glass that rests in my hand.

I discovered it a few days after my father telephoned from Mexico to say he has decided to stay there until he dies. "I'm not long for this world. I need you to ship me some things," he said, so I reached for the notepad next to my computer and took down his requests, an itemized list that would trigger my weeklong scavenger hunt inside his unoccupied Central California home, my discovery of this particular scorpion specimen bottled on the shelf above his desk—and my subsequent thievery. Although my father built a career, a life, around his research on the evolution of arachnids—spiders, mites, and scorpions—he made no mention of his specimen collection the day he rattled his list into the receiver.

"The Great Courses DVD collection, and the most recent catalogue from The Teaching Company," he said. His voice cracked with urgency. "My *Encyclopedia Britannica* set, including the annual almanacs. Posters of Blue Boy and Pinkie—the reproductions I got last year at the Huntington Museum, not the photocopies in my bedroom, but the original posters. You'll have to remove them from the frames."

With the phone clamped between my shoulder and jaw, I repeated the list back to him.

He added a few more items, then proceeded to describe in utmost detail where each object could be found inside his house.

"I know where it all is," I said several times, and "Yes, of course I know that too." His house is just five doors down from mine and I know the layout quite well. But he didn't stop no matter how many *I knows* I uttered, because once he gets going on a train of thought it's impossible for him to stop. Impossible.

After a while I doodled on the notepad, saying "uh-huh" every few seconds.

My father had gone to Irapuato, Mexico, at my urging. A few months earlier, my brother David and I had bought him a one-way ticket with the vague promise of a return flight at his convenience. We hoped that without a specific return date, he might be more inclined to stay longer than three weeks—perhaps forever. This isn't quite as harsh as it seems. For decades my dad has dreamed of moving there permanently, surrounded by the language and landscape he loves, the deserts and beaches and mountains where he gathered arachnid specimens for half a century. He also has extended family there: his deceased wife's family, and my brother David's family, including my sister-in-law Penny and their two young girls. He would be near lots of relatives who could look after him. Relatives other than me. Far, far away.

Among the things he requested were his *Great Books of the Western World*, a hardbound series published in 1952, fifty-four volumes covering classic literature, including works of fiction, history, natural science, philosophy, mathematics, and religion. I didn't tell him that the information contained in these books is readily available on the Internet, or that it would be cheaper for him to mail order new books and have them sent directly to his apartment in Mexico. He doesn't use computers, and anyway, once he sets his mind to something, he disregards all other options.

"On the bookcase next to my bed," he said. As always, he over-pronounced his words: /book-kās/ with a double k sound, /nek-st / in two syllables.

"Yes, I know."

"I must have them with me. They are monumental works by and about great authors. The most influential thinkers of our time."

I know, I know, I fucking know. But I did not say this either, because I've long understood that once he gets started he cannot stop. Cannot.

"Be sure to include the supplemental texts on Aristotle. Aristotle lived from 384 BC until 322 BC. He was a student of Plato and he taught Alexander the Great."

My father's speech patterns—his vocabulary and syntax—are unusually formal. Classic Asperger's, from what I understand, albeit undiagnosed. His mannerisms certainly balance on the edge of the autism spectrum. Strained social interaction, repetitive patterns of behavior, hyper focus on specific interests—these traits manifest themselves as tiny droplets of personality toxins, not fatal, but unpleasant.

I doodled through his monologue on Plato and the dates of Chaucer and Sir Francis Bacon.

Also on his list: five pairs of leather shoes, four new suits, a case of unopened vitamin supplements, odor-free garlic tablets, a carton of bottles labeled ALL NATURAL MALE ENHANCEMENT, a small leather-bound address book, back issues of *Scientific American*, and several file folders of correspondence—each labeled by name—one marked STEPHEN JAY GOULD.

"I'll be so grateful for you to send me these things, Carole."

"Uh-huh."

"I'm on the line between life and death. These things will keep me alive longer, do you understand?"

I suppose I said the things one is expected to say to a father. I suppose I said, *Don't be silly. You're not dying anytime soon,* or *Stop talking such nonsense,* or *But I thought you'd live to be one hundred and five—remember your plan? You're only eighty-two, so you have twenty-three years to go.* Or maybe I didn't say those things, but thought them instead. Our conversations are so cyclical, the topics so recurrent, including his ever-immediately impending death—which he's been predicting for some forty years now—that I often lose track of what I've specifically said on which day.

I cradled the phone against my jaw and bulleted each item with little curly-cues. In that moment I wasn't sure if I was a good daughter or a bad one. I said the things a daughter should say, carried out actions expected of me, took dictation, wrote the list—but part of me considered throwing the list away, folding it in half and letting it go in the breeze outside. While my father prepared for his final respite by gathering earthly items of comfort and interest, things to make his remaining life enjoyable, I wasn't sure I wanted to deliver. Perhaps if I withheld his treasures he would postpone his passage from this world—stave off death—in which case my inclination to tear up the list was morally just. On the other hand, my withholding would cause him some degree of discomfort. I could let him squirm down there in Mexico—waiting and waiting for his things that would never arrive—pinch him with passive-aggressive retaliation for my accumulated list of his past transgressions, a fuzzy litany I haven't fully articulated even to myself. Good daughter or bad? Perhaps I was both in that moment, a morally liminal creature with one foot on each side.

"Are you getting this all down?" he asked.

Four

Hordes of specimen jars once filled both my father's offices, one at the university where he taught in Southern California and a second study at home. Years after my parents split, he lived for a while in a double-wide mobile home in Chino where the hollow floor shook if you stepped too heavily, sending vibrations up the walls and rattling rows of specimen jars on their plywood shelves. When I was a teenager, visiting during the summer, I once slammed the door on purpose just to watch my friend Lana's reaction as the scorpions fluttered momentarily to life, their legs and pincers gently rising in rippling isopropyl tides sloshing rim to rim. I laughed when her shoulders instinctually flapped up and down in heebie-jeebie, get-them-off-me reflex. Her mouth contorted to expose her clenched teeth and she involuntarily bent forward to slap her bare shins repeatedly, as if the reptilian, survival part of her brain were unable to differentiate between real and imagined threats. While I now know that her reactive behavior typifies our genetic predisposition to fear animals that once posed a danger to ancient humans (as you can see, I've inherited some of my father's diction), I reveled in the in-between moment of unspoken what-ifs racing at lightning speed behind Lana's wide eyes, the what-should-I-do hypothetical scenario playing out in her head as her hypothalamus and sensory cortex conversed, assessing the repercussion of every decision should these scorpions be alive and loose.

Suppose you were bitten by a scorpion. Let's say the Deathstalker, *Apistobuthus pterygocercus*. The initial sting feels like several bee stings at once. You cry out in pain, then kick your foot into the air to jolt the scorpion from your ankle. Your heart races, banging furiously against your sternum; has the scorpion's venom caused your heart to pound, or is this merely a psychological reaction, you wonder. You linger for a few minutes, suspended in inaction, indecision—should you seek medical attention or just let the pain in your ankle subside? Let's say you wait it out. No need for drama. Scorpion stings are overrated, overplayed—the stories of agonizing deaths are urban legends grown to monstrosities, you reason. So you apply an ice pack to ease the pain in your ankle, the red circle radiating from the point of contact. Your heart pounds harder. Blood thrushes against your eardrums. You feel hot. You start to sweat. You close your eyes, lean back on the couch, and elevate your ankle with a pile of throw pillows. As neurotoxins surge through your brain, they clamp onto sodium channels, alternately blocking and activating signals to your nervous system.

The first convulsions take you by surprise—your arms tremble, your feet tingle, your lower abdomen contracts several times, like a shiver but stronger. You're neither moving your body nor are you still, you think; you quake on the threshold of voluntary physical action and involuntary reaction. It's time to seek help, so you look at the phone a few feet away; but within just this sliver of time, the time you took to contemplate your situation, paralysis has crept in. Your eyelids slam back in their utmost open position, your eyeballs halt, trapped in a frozen gaze, and your limbs, trembling, flop up and down with the rhythm of your heaving torso as it folds and unfolds like a piece of paper trapped in the wind. Finally your blood pressure drops and muscles release, loose again. The last thing you see is the telephone nestled uselessly in its cradle, and as fluid secretions seep into your lungs and pain-killing endorphins flood your brain, you welcome the coma, the sleep, the flood of deep relaxation that feels so, so good.

Five

The day after my father's phone call I began packing his books. The volumes on his list represent only a fraction of his library, so although I knew generally where to look in each room for specific titles, I opened all the blinds and doors to allow as much light into the house as possible. February's winter chill wafted in from the front and back yards, and although I intended to work quickly and with big body movements in order to stave off the cold, I found myself lingering, occasionally pausing to open certain books. At first my curiosity was random—pull a book, crack it open, notice a word or two, slide it into the open banker's box on the floor. I lifted *The Rites of Passage*, originally published in 1908, reprinted in 1960. The pages smelled of dust, of moisture. I read. Pondered. Reached for the dictionary to look something up, then the encyclopedia, then back to *The Rites of Passage*, then reached for something else, losing myself in a linked meandering of then-and-then, piling open books on the carpet around me rather than filling the cardboard box.

My digressive thread—liminality: The condition of being on a threshold or at the beginning of a process. To be *in "limbo,"* says anthropologist Arnold van Gennep, *is to inhabit an intermediate, ambivalent zone.* In liminal phase an individual experiences a blurring of social environment and reality, occupies the in-between stage. The term derives from the Latin *limen*, which means *boundary, transitional mark, passage between two different places. Liminal space represents a threshold of a physiological or psychological response,* the place where you teeter between action and inaction, the moment you consider calling for help; the instant your eyes dart between the phone and the red spot spreading from your ankle; the window of time between your last inhalation and your first convulsion—and there it is, the sliver of time that precedes paralysis, a sliver so fine, so sharp it defies balance. You must step off, onto one side or the other. Go or stay; float or sink; here or there. Which way will you lean?

And what can I say to ease your fear, dear father, alleviate your angst: *one hundred and five, remember the plan?* Or maybe I should give you a push instead, tell you to count backward from eighty-two and let your abdomen sink, rest on the smooth glass bottom. When the lid turns to seal the portal, the flood will feel so, so good. Liminality: *The psychological point beyond which a sensation becomes too faint to be experienced.*

By noon, the liminal hour between morning's lingering chill and afternoon's oncoming warmth, the neighborhood outside my father's silent front door chirped with sounds of life. I looked up from whichever book I held and walked to the window. Two young mothers from around the block pushed strollers side by side in the street as a preschooler rode his bicycle alongside them on the sidewalk, his rear tire balanced unsteadily but safely between two spinning plastic training wheels. I imagine that if that little boy were to fall, if the training wheels failed to keep him upright, he would not hesitate to cry out for help, and his mother would rush to his aid, either tilting the bike upright to get him back on track or scooping him up off the ground should he topple to the concrete.

I remember the first time I rode a two-wheeler, a secondhand blue-and-white Schwinn my parents had picked up at Leroy's

Thrift Store in Pomona the winter of my first-grade year. I don't recall my father being present for that particular rite of passage, the day I learned to ride a bike. He wasn't the type to ride bikes, play ball, or attend Open House at my elementary school, but preferred instead to hole up in his study alone, or engage a few of his students in deep intellectual debate while smoking pot under the fig tree in our backyard. Lana was there the day of my inaugural lesson, though, along with a gaggle of neighborhood kids. One of the tall boys from the apartments across the street instructed me while the other kids huddled around. We stood at the interior end of my parents' driveway, a long concrete corridor shaded by thick mulberry trees and the slatted-wood carport covering, a structure my father had built the preceding fall. The tall boy braced the bike upright as I climbed into place and rested my feet on the pedals. The other kids all shouted instructions at me as I sat on the wide leather seat, still unmoving, still braced, aimed toward sunny Ninth Street at the other end of the dark driveway.

"Ready?" the tall boy asked.

I didn't answer right away. I paused. A moment of indecision.

The kids' voices swirled past my ears, making little sense to me at that moment—advice on which way to lean, how to grip the handlebars, how pressing backward on the pedals would engage the coaster brake. One voice I did hear, though. "We'll catch you if you fall," someone said.

"All set?" the boy asked again.

I nodded.

On the count of three the boy gave me a push. At first I teetered, overcorrecting the handlebars several times, wrenching them side to side. But as I gained forward momentum I finally straightened out the front wheel. I found the sweet spot, the arrow-like glide. Balance. Exactly in between left and right. *Lean. Let up. Lean.* My friends ran alongside as I rolled toward the light, still solely propelled by the force of the tall boy's push, through the darkened corridor toward the bright open space where the sidewalk divided our place from everyplace else, a concrete boundary separating Insulated-In-Here from Risk-Laden-Out-There.

I think it was Lana who finally screamed for me to pedal.

I pumped my right foot down, then my left. The bike burst forward, powered past the voices and scampering feet, and sailed into the open, wide street hot with sunlight and possibility.

Six

My father's absence that afternoon is representative of so many absences, a single line item in my catalogue of his inattentive moments and self-sequestered years. Even when he was around, he wasn't *really* around.

The day of my birth (which, coincidentally, fell on his thirty-sixth birthday) marked the beginning of our shared lives. Over the years, I've pieced together the story of my tenuous origin. My father often tells the part about racing my mother to the hospital before dawn the morning of his birthday, the second of June. When my mother started to crown right there in the elevator, the nurses ushered her directly into the delivery room. He paced the waiting room with bated breath, his mind wild with possibilities, good and bad. On one hand, he says, he was eager for the baby, the skin and bone manifestation of his DNA, his contribution to human-kind's evolution. On the other hand, he wrestled with worry and guilt about how the baby might turn out.

My father admits that when they first learned of my mother's pregnancy he wasn't at all happy. Something had to be done. "There are doctors that handle this," he said to my mother. What he still doesn't know is that on the day of her scheduled pregnancy termination, my mother returned home without having gone to the clinic. My mother tells me she lied to my father, claiming she'd received a hypertonic saline injection but the six-week embryo didn't abort. "I guess we're stuck," she told him.

Seven and a half months later, my father paced the delivery waiting room and wondered how that super-salt shot might have mangled the gestating fetus. Would this baby be physically deformed or mentally affected? A hell of a price to pay, he thought.

Finally the doctor emerged from the delivery room, smiley-faced at twenty-two minutes past six: "It's a girl," he said. "Congratulations, Bruce."

At my mother's bedside, my father carefully balanced my head in the fleshy crook of his folded arm, and when he had counted all ten fingers for the third time, his eyes watered and he told my mother how perfect we both were, she and me.

My father usually omits from his recounting that within days of bringing me home, my baby noises were too much of a distraction to his studies, so he erected a tent for my mother and me in the backyard, the large army-green canvas shelter they'd used on my father's scorpion-gathering expeditions in the Mexican desert. I know this may be hard to believe, but I shit you not, dear reader. There on the dry Bermuda grass, with a lawn chair inched to the edge of a Woolworth's plastic wading pool, a pair of foot-high camping cots, and a floor fan powered by an extension cord stretching back to the house, my nineteen-year-old mother tended me during the days, her red-faced newborn, cooing, crying, nursing, and sleeping through the summer heat.

The photos from that time, at least as I remember them, paint a deceptively simple picture. I've seen only a few snapshots from those days, and it has been many years since I've seen them, so the image in my mind is a bit fuzzy. All appears relatively serene through the camera lens—a hippie-ish scene with my mother smiling from behind the frames of her cat-eye glasses; my father bare-chested and barefoot in dress slacks cut off above the knee. I imagine them taking turns holding their new infant there in the yard, snapping a camera loaded with a fresh roll of Kodak slide film and sipping sun tea flavored with fresh lemon wedges picked from the side yard. He probably took several little breaks like this over the course of the day, walking back and forth from the living room to the yard. Then in the evening, when the sun sank beneath the neighborhood's drooping power lines, my mother joined my father in the house for spaghetti and sliced cantaloupe. My mother slept with me inside the house at night and returned to the back-yard campsite each morning.

No, he wasn't exactly cruel, at least not intentionally. He just wasn't all that interested in fatherhood. Many people don't really want to be parents; rather, parenthood sort of happens to them. We all deal with it in our unique ways. Some of us learn to balance personal need with responsibility and end up enjoying it. Others meet their responsibilities and mask their disdain, sometimes successfully, other times not. Perhaps it's a manifestation of the Asperger's, but my father rarely camouflages his intentions. If he doesn't want children he simply says so—to me, to anyone, with neither hesitation nor vexed emotional tone—then tells his pregnant wife to make an appointment at the clinic. If the crying baby bothers his reading, again he simply says so, then rummages through the garage until he finds the tent poles. Does this prove him one or the other, either a good or bad father? In isolation, no, I don't think so. But when does the cumulative factor enter the algorithm? On one side of the equation, he missed pretty much all of my rites of passage. Never did he attend (or even know about, in most cases) a parent conference, open house, graduation, swim meet, driving lesson, birthday party, marching parade, or music recital.

On the other side of the equation, I remember the morning he rushed to my rescue during the San Fernando earthquake of

1971—which rumbled from its epicenter fifty miles northwest of Pomona—just weeks after I'd learned to ride my bike, the same year he would capture the scorpion I have recently stolen. Asleep in the top bunk in my bedroom (I'm not sure why we had bunk beds at that time, as my brother would have been less than a year old and still sleeping in a crib in my parents' room), I was awakened by the clank-clank-clank of the head- and footboards rattling erratically. I sank my head deeper into the pillow and drifted back to sleep for maybe a second or two, incorporating the side-to-side rocking motion of the bunk bed into the dream I'd been having, until the noise in my dream thumped louder, then took on weight, cannoning past the pit of my stomach. My eyes slammed open with instantaneous focus. The whole bunk bed teetered away from the wall. The force threw me against the outer guardrail, which stopped me from rolling off the edge. Then abruptly the bed swung back the other way, ramming against the wall so hard it popped the guardrail up and out of its shallow niche, hurling it across the room like a giant scorpion tail in full attack. The top bunk arched away from the wall again, farther out this time. Without hesitation I sat straight up, turned away from the wall and leaned back, against the bed's outward momentum. If the bed had been the front tire of a wobbly bike, my body was the handlebar: *Lean. Let up. Lean.* Back and forth the bunk frame shuddered while tiny bits of plaster rained from the ceiling. Just as the window next to my headboard pinged, then cracked, my father burst through the door in his underwear. He pushed the bed up against the wall with all his weight. He wedged himself at an angle, a human plank, with arms outstretched, palms pushing upward against my mattress, his bare toes curled into the rug for traction.

"I gotcha," he said.

We rode out the earthquake like that, him leaning into the bunk frame, me leaning backward into the wall. I had no idea at the time, and wouldn't fully understand until years later, that during those moments the world outside our house crumbled. I didn't know what Richter 6.6 meant or that sixty-five people would die that day. While twelve bridges fell onto highway lanes, two hospitals collapsed, an entire medical center heaved off its foundation, and the lower section of the Van Norman Dam crumbled, my father and I found the sweet spot, the upright balance, if only for a few slow-motion seconds. We managed to leverage our bodies against the shifting continent below us. While the Earth's crust transitioned—buckled and split and sank—my father and I inhabited a fleeting moment of limbo. We countered the vibrations pulsing through the wood floor on its raised, hollow foundation.

While my shoulder blades thumped against the wall, I watched over my father's bare shoulder as the crack in the window grew longer and more complex, ascending upward at a slight diagonal and splintering off like a windblown bush, or a tree permanently etched on the horizon.

Forty years later, I looked through the screened window of my father's vacant home some three hundred miles north of my childhood Pomona house, going through his things. Outside, the little boy continued riding his bike down the sidewalk, his plastic training wheels pinging with grit and gravel fragments. He pumped the pedals hard several times, then turned his head to look at his mother as he glided past her. She didn't seem to notice his daring feat, deep in conversation with her friend, so he hooted, "Look at me!"

She turned and raised her fist in way-to-go encouragement.

I moved to my father's desk in the office, a converted room at the back of the house. There I found seven old specimen jars with spiders, mites, crabs, and scorpions. One jar had long ago shattered in place; the spider, no longer preserved, lay dried and crumbled amid shards of glass. It occurred to me then, not for the first time, how little I understand of my father, yet how quickly time narrows the boundaries of our shared earthy existence—soon he'll be gone. It's not the chronology of his life that evades me. I know much of what he did and when, despite the fact that he was intermittently absent from my life until he moved to my town, my neighborhood, a few years ago. Although I've read much about the high-functioning edge of the autism spectrum—the lack of empathy, intense preoccupation with a particular subject, one-sided verbosity, impaired emotional reciprocity—part of me still can't understand why his work was so important to him, why his intellectual life took precedence over our family.

Wait. I take that back. Truth be told, I actually do understand *why* he is the way he is. What I wonder is why *I* ended up with such a parent.

Seven

Over Thanksgiving dinner in my living room last November, he said again—in the exact same words, same intonation, same cadence as the hundred times before—how lucky we are to exist at all. How fortunate we humans are to be alive, let alone sentient. While the rest of us at the table talked about mundane things—about road construction blocking the downtown freeway exit, and which alternative route might be best over the next few weeks—he interrupted with his own train of thought.

"The probability of the existence of your individual, unique genome is about one over a googolplex," he blurted to no one in particular, but looked at my mother-in-law.

"Oh," she said, not knowing how else to respond. She reached for her soda and puckered her lips around the straw.

"Do you know what a googolplex is?" he said to everyone, but looked at me.

"No," I said on cue.

"Do you want to know?"

"Sure." Still on cue.

"It can be represented in a mathematical equation."

The table thus quieted, he lifted a pen and three-by-five-inch notepad from his breast pocket. He wrote: $10(10)(100)$. "Or it can be written out as a number. A googolplex is the second largest number with a name. It's a one, followed by a googol of zeros."

He paused.

"Do you know how much a googol is?" he finally asked.

My cue again. "How much?"

He explained that a googol is the number ten raised to the hundredth power, which is presumed to be greater than the number of atoms in the observable universe. A googolplex, then, is the number ten to the power of googol. It would be impossible for a person to print all the zeros in a googolplex because there isn't enough space in the known universe. And it would take more than a googol years for that person to write out all those zeros. "It's impossible to visualize how big a googolplex is," he said.

My mother-in-law said nothing, just nodded politely and pushed the mashed potatoes with her fork.

"You had a one-in-a-googolplex chance of being here today," he said.

Very long pause. We all teetered on the threshold of awkward silence. I wondered if I should let the moment settle, or if I should say something to alleviate the social pain I imagined my guests felt. Let it die, or rescue it?

And then, before I decided what to say, he mended the moment himself. "Carole, would you please be kind enough to pass the salt?"

The likelihood of our existence, of everything around us, in fact—all life on Earth—has been the subject of much scholarly discourse. In his book *Wonderful Life*, Harvard paleontologist Stephen Jay Gould describes bio-evolution as a copiously branching bush that originated by an improbable accumulation of accidental contingencies. Gould posits that if the evolutionary tape were played again, there is no way to predict what would happen— and no reason to expect that humans would exist at all. He later explains in an interview with *Time* magazine, "It is like *Back to the Future*. In the movie, Doc Brown goes to a blackboard and draws a chart. The top line is history as it actually occurred. But if you make this teeny little change, which is Biff Tannen getting that sports almanac, then history veers off. It isn't that it is random that it happened the second way.... It's just that what actually happened is one of a billion possible alternatives, and you'd never get it to run exactly the same way again."

Eight

There in my father's office, next to the crumbled spider and shards of broken glass on his desk, the tail of the *Paruroctonus silvestrii* leaned against the inner wall of its narrow circular tomb. *Las Estacas, Mexico—1971*, the label said. The jar, two and a half inches tall and one inch in diameter, stood upright like a coffin set on end. The scorpion inside was positioned head down, tail up with its abdomen and front claws slouched unnaturally in the bottom corner. I wondered that afternoon as I went through his things, and I still wonder now, what the scorpion reveals—what it might tell me about my father's life's work, about my father himself. About the connection between my father and myself.

I tipped the jar on its side so the scorpion rested more naturally flat.

For the scorpion, its last day alive might have gone like this: With its two fighting claws thrust forward in guardian stance, the *Paruroctonus silvestrii* emerged with a dry rustle from a finger-sized hole under the rock. In the center of a patch of packed earth it balanced on the tips of its four pairs of legs, nerves and muscles braced for action. Hair-like protrusions on its legs quarried for vibrations, minute air movements which would determine its next move—attack or retreat.

Normally the scorpion would not come out of its burrow during the day, but an overcast sky pushed inland from the Pacific and toggled between light and dark, creating a twilight effect the scorpion mistook for dusk. In a dome of shade cast by the rock, its two-inch yellow body glinted where the moist brown stinger protruded from the last segment of the tail, now arched over, parallel with the scorpion's flat back. Slowly the stinger slid from its sheath. The nerves in the poison sac relaxed.

A few feet away, at the base of a yucca, a small, oblivious beetle trudged nearer. The scorpion's down-slope rush gave him no time to spread his wings. The beetle's legs quivered in protest as the sharp claw snapped round his body. The stinger lanced into him from over the scorpion's head. The beetle teetered between life and death for the slightest instant, then stilled.

The scorpion stood motionless for several minutes, pausing to identify its dead prey and retest the ground and air for hostile vibrations. Confident, its claw retracted from the half-severed beetle and its two small feeding pincers stretched forward to pierce the beetle's flesh.

Deliberately and methodically the scorpion ate its victim.

An hour later, as it slowly sucked the last morsels of beetle flesh off its pincers, the signal for the scorpion's own death went undetected from behind the yucca—faint sounds audible to a human, but vibrations just outside the range of the scorpion's sensory system.

A few feet away, a freckled hand with uneven, dirty fingernails raised an overturned glass jar.

The scorpion felt a tiny ripple in the air. At once its fighting claws hoisted and groped. Its stinger was erect in the rigid tail, its nearsighted eyes staring up for the enemy.

The jar came down. From underneath, a heavy index card slid between the scorpion and the sand, and with one swift move the man flipped the jar and the card upright, then upside down again, dropping the scorpion into a second jar filled with formaldehyde. The scorpion clawed at the glass walls, writhed sideways and up. Submerged, it strained for the surface, snapped again at the walls, again down, again up, until finally its convulsions slowed.

Still squatting, the man slipped the index card into his breast pocket. When the scorpion's stinger finally relaxed and its pincers floated peacefully to either side, the man stood, rubbed his hands down the sides of his pants, and stepped past the yucca toward the road. In the echoing silence a cicada clickity-zinged from inside the thorny bush; below, an anxious lizard scuttled between leaves as dry and thin as molted snakeskin.

Nine

Over the next several days I ravaged my father's personal belongings. I burrowed through drawers, cupboards, shelves, boxes, organizer trays, envelopes, cabinets, files, magazine stacks, grade books, checkbook registers, ornamental covered dishes, pockets, hampers, bills, memos, letters, receipts, journals, jars, crystal bowls, plastic containers. At some point my mission to collect the items he'd requested morphed into something else.

How would I feel if he died today? We had shared homes, off and on, the first ten years of my life. Then we lived three hundred miles apart, visiting once a year at most, until a few years back he moved to the town I live in. In some respects, I hardly know this man. In other ways, I can anticipate his every move. What label describes our relationship? And would I regret not knowing him better—or could I at least appreciate him more if I understood him from a different perspective?

Alone in his house, I pinched and clawed through his things. I wanted to know what my father sought in scorpions—if I could make meaning of his work, perhaps that would balance the equation for me; justify the uneven weight of family man versus scholar, intellect versus emotional connection. Snooping through his personal things was a way of getting closer to the man I consciously held at arm's length, while rooting out his unsavory secrets would help me justify my ongoing participation in our father-daughter dance of disconnection. Intimacy from a safe distance. My eyes and fingers quarried for minute insights that would determine my stance as a daughter—poised to deliver the itemized goods, or reconciled to withhold his treasures? Let him squirm, perhaps. I am not proud of my actions. But I was driven. Even if I had wanted to cease my search, it would have been impossible to stop. Impossible.

As an adult I recognize many qualities in myself that I also see in my father, some good, some bad. I think most of us can say that about our parents. So how do we distinguish between good parenting and bad? Good daughters and bad? If our life experiences contribute to determining the adults we become, and if some seemingly negative experiences germinate some sort of timely lesson, then how are we to judge the actions of our parents—of ourselves, of anyone—with black and white clarity? Each action, each event, each nuance of life introduces new variables, new risks, new possibilities. Perhaps the tall boy from the apartments across the street pushed my Schwinn bike with a slightly different velocity or angle than my father would have, or maybe Lana would not have been as shy around my father as she had been in the presence of the handsome, tall boy; had it been my father giving the lesson, perhaps Lana wouldn't have waited so long to shout her instructions for me to pedal—in which case my bike riding experience might have evolved into a different lesson than the one I came away with that day, something other than how to compensate for a series of over-corrections, which weeks later translated to my intuitive strategy for counterbalancing the teetering bunk bed. Or perhaps I would have eventually learned the exact overcompensation counterbalance lesson under my father's instruction, but too late to help me during the earth-quake on February 9, 1971. Who knows?

I wonder about the scorpion in the jar. If the evolutionary tape were played again in Las Estacas, Mexico, that hot July day in 1971, which variables would remain constant and which con-tingencies, if altered, would have prompted the scorpion to act differently? And what repercussions might that have had for the scorpion? For the beetle? My father? One changed variable might set in motion another chain of reactions, a chain which may have altered the scorpion's fate. Or my father's. Or mine. Suppose the scorpion had stung my father. Suppose he died in the Mexican desert that day. Or suppose he lived, but was so shaken that he de-cided to change his career path. What if he had stayed in Pomona to read children's books aloud to me on the sofa instead of driving twenty-five hundred miles cross-country to present his research to Harvard medical students?

Gould, of course, is right—there is no way to predict what would happen. Even if we could change a particular variable in the past, the chain reaction of possible outcomes alters the very structure of the branching bush. I wonder how far each leaf reaches, how wide the circle of our apparent spheres of influence.

During one of my scavenger-hunt days inside my father's home, around dusk, a neighbor called to his dogs in the front yard, clinked tools on the driveway. He seemed to be looking my way, looking toward the window where I stood, where I scoured and pilfered. I stepped aside and reached for the plastic wand. Twist, twist, and the blinds tilted in unison, fluttered closed like the gills of a giant, hungry fish.

Ten

During the years I taught third grade, my students often picked scorpions as the topic for their independent research projects. A socially defiant but exceptionally bright boy named Tyler hunkered behind a barricade of several large hardbound books propped upright on his desk during sustained silent reading time one afternoon. He loved the close-up photographs depicting spine-like tail segments, nearly transparent abdomen cuticles, and elongated pincers. Earlier in the year I'd figured out that if I wanted Tyler to keep reading something, I had to feign disapproval— otherwise, he instantly lost interest in the topic and redirected his attention to something else, like flinging straight-pin-spiked spit wads across the room with a makeshift slingshot fashioned from a stolen pencil and his deskmate's hair scrunchie.

"What'cha reading?" I asked.

Tyler lowered one of the books. He smiled at me through squinted eyes and pointed to an enlarged image of one scorpion cannibalizing another.

"Gross," I said. "Why do they do that?"

"The females eat the males after they mate."

"Yuck."

"So cool."

"I think you should put this away. And if there's a chapter on giant sea scorpions from the dinosaur days, don't read that, either. Have you heard about ancient scorpion monsters? I wonder if it's true. Never mind. You'll have nightmares."

As I walked away Tyler flipped to the index at the back of the book, then spent the rest of the afternoon, including the time he should have been participating in a social studies lesson, scribbling in a notebook resting covertly on his lap.

To the horror and gleeful fascination of his classmates, a week or so later, Tyler delivered his oral report, which explained that 400 million years ago, ten-foot-long giant sea scorpions violently reigned at the top of the food chain. "They grew so big because there was a lot of oxygen in the air," he said, and then went on to explain that large fish, more fierce than the giant sea scorpions, forced the scorpions onto land, where they evolved back to a smaller size. "They went from small to huge to tiny," he said, holding up a picture he'd drawn, a comic book–type scene with one scorpion biting off another scorpion's head, while nearby a fang-jawed shark-looking creature dripped anticipatory globs of saliva from its tongue.

"Any questions?" Tyler asked.

Hands shot up.

When I was a kid, my father led graduate students through the sand dunes of Baja to collect all manner of arachnids during university-sponsored field trips. I imagine they hiked among the yuccas, and when my father paused to speak in his undulating rhythm of overly pronounced words, longhaired twenty-somethings scribbled furiously in their notebooks.

I recall one particular drive through the Mexican desert in our Volkswagen camper van with the music blaring, the windows down. I was around seven years old, small enough to stand upright on the floorboard between the driver and passenger seats. My father loosely fingered the steering wheel with one hand while his other hand rested on the gearshift knob. I swayed left-right-left in the growing, liminal gap between my parents as the van shimmied side to side from the vibrations of the tires. My mother mouthed the words to Biff Rose's "Buzz the Fuzz" while I balanced barefoot beside her. I could have easily toppled over, but I kept my center of gravity low, like a scorpion braced for action, my legs slightly bent. With my bare thighs safely cradled against the armrests of the two seats, I danced. *Lean. Let up. Lean.* I danced with knees limber, danced to keep myself upright, danced in the hot Mexican wind like a folded piece of blank paper, flapping, free.

Years after my parents divorced, when I had grown into the door-slamming teenager who laughed at my friend's heebie-jeebie reactions to a room full of dead bugs, my father often tried to explain the nature of his work to me—some of which I understood, but mostly not. The problem was that he spoke to me in the only language he seemed capable of, which was the same language he used in his university lectures and scholarly publications. In 1973 he published a paper in the *Journal of Arachnology* on the evolution of the arachnid internal skeleton and its relationship to the evolution of the circulatory system. In this paper, he suggests "the neoteny as the major mechanism to explain the origin of the non-scorpion arachnids from scorpion ancestors." Among other things, he details his discovery of what he calls "a perineural vascular membrane of certain lungless, rare arachnids."

In bits and pieces, I am slowly coming to comprehend some of the theoretical significance of his discoveries regarding the anatomy of the scorpions he collected during those trips. To paraphrase (and oversimplify) his words: tracing the changes of arachnid anatomy (specifically the circulatory system) through both fossil records and modern-day specimens provides evidence to support the evolution of ancient sea scorpions into many various modern-day spiders and scorpions. I glean from his research that, as sea scorpions evolved from gill-breathing swimmers to lung-breathing land walkers to vascular-membrane-breathers (with non-functional lungs), they were indeed liminal creatures.

Eleven

Among the items my father asked me to send him is a file folder containing his once-ongoing correspondence with Stephen Jay Gould. While fishing for Gould's file among several four-drawer filing cabinets that line the walls of my father's study, I discovered that the drawers hold hundreds of manila folders, each labeled and alphabetized by last name. Apparently, my father was quite the letter writer. Not only did he write hundreds, perhaps thousands of letters over his lifetime, but he kept copies of many of the letters he wrote as well as those he received. I don't know why he did this. It could have been part of his compulsion to collect, inventory, and categorize things.

After days of rifling his files, it began to appear to me that he has been documenting his life. Perhaps he anticipated his future value to the academic world would merit the preservation of his every printed word, both personal and professional. Poised for fame. Or posthumous recognition. I know that Thomas Jefferson copied everything he wrote, too; he used a cumbersome duplicating machine that produced a copy of a piece of writing simultaneously via a set of parallel pens attached to an elaborate configuration of wooden boxes. As a prolific letter writer and timely archivist, Jefferson managed to document his viewpoints and insights so that we could study his ideas long after his death. Perhaps my father was creating a body of work to be studied after his death, too. Or maybe the archive I retrieved from his office is a manifestation of his narrow yet multi-branched intensity. His groping on the edge of a neurological spectrum.

It had been several days since my father called with his list. Technically, I had everything he'd requested, but still I holed up in my father's office. I scrutinized the files for hours, reading under a dim lamp while the sky outside turned black. I randomly pulled letters, one after another. When I look back on those hours now, I see myself as if through the wide-angle lens of an old camera mounted near the ceiling, a grainy image I have contrived in my mind: In the photo's frame, I straddle the open sliding-glass door that separates the house from the backyard; I stand, papers in hand, with one foot on each side of the threshold; in the light, I will deliver—fulfill the request made of me by gathering items on a list; in the dark, I scavenge—search for meaning. I traversed the line between intimacy and emotional distance, empathy and resentment, self-serving voyeurism and objective observation. Good daughter or bad? More to the point, does the motivation justify the behavior?

As I kneeled before an open drawer my eyes rested on a file name: *Rolf Lyon*. I remember Rolf from my childhood—a pre-med biology student who became a good friend of my father. He often camped with us in Las Estacas, patiently threading marshmallows on a wire for me, then blowing out the flames when they would inevitably catch fire. The letters in the folder span 1964 to 1999.

April 4, 1977

Dear Rolf,

...I've been sort of depressed lately because it seems to me that I haven't accomplished anything important in my career as a professor. When I was your age I thought that by the time I was my age I would

either be dead or else a world-famous zoologist. Well, I'm 48 and still
alive and nobody.

So my father, too, struggled to find meaning and purpose in
his work. And to think, all these years I'd assumed him to be so
self-certain. At the time he wrote this letter he was close to my age
now. I understand his angst. The question gnaws at me, too. I've
often wondered if and when I'll make it, and if the value of my
life's work will appreciate or depreciate over time. For those of us
who don't have children, how do we contribute to mankind's evolution if not through the passage of our genetic material? It seems
so obvious to me that my father's academic accomplishments were
indeed worthy, that asking about the natural world may not
result in definitive answers, much less fame—but the value is in
the asking, the search that leads from one question to the next,
like a ripple on the ocean's surface that swells toward the quaking
continental shelf, then crashes on the sand before pulling into itself
again. All intellectual thought, all humanistic notions of education
are based on the act of questioning. Socrates asked questions; his
form of inquiry rippled debate between individuals with opposing
viewpoints; it was the asking and responding that stimulated criti-
cal thinking, illuminated ideas. Plato asked. Aristotle asked. Ideas
swelled, evolved into sub-ideas of related origin, answered or not.
Modern scholars, giants in their fields of expertise, joined the
collective discourse as it stretched upward, arched and curled with
too many voices to distinguish one from another—scientists and
spiritual leaders and laypersons and your next-door neighbor. My
father. Me. My third-grade students. My current students at the
university. Our ideas, our wonderings rush toward the shore and
crash in on one another. Temporary chaos ensues. A beautiful
cacophony of seaweed and salt that splays, then draws back to
rejoin the huge body of water that pulls into itself again and again.

In a 1989 letter to Dr. Gould, my father says of his own research and discovery:

> *This supports the macro-evolutionary aspects of punctuated equilibrium theory. It is my current belief that all macro-evolutionary novelties arise from the mutations of regulatory genes that cause changes in developmental timing. These allometric changes in body proportions can either be localized or else generalized. The mutations occur randomly, of course, but they do not need to be immediately advantageous; they only need to be viable. They can be carried in the gene pool until such time as they are favored fortuitously by environmental selection pressures, at which time their frequencies will be increased in the gene pool because of differential reproduction rates.*

In other words, the reason certain anatomical features of modern scorpions matter is because this evidence supports the theory of evolution—especially aspects of Darwin's theory that have been the focus of dispute by evolution-oppositionists. So by providing evidence of scorpion evolution, my father aimed to fill in one small blank spot in Darwin's argument.

Today's discourse on evolution teeters betwixt and between the known and the unknown; consideration of either side of the debate, either creationist or evolutionist, invites you to temporarily occupy an intermediate position, a liminal space—linger on the damp Mexican shore that bisects land and sea. This gives me pause: If research yields no immediate answer to humankind's inquiry of nature (or of God, for that matter), does that mean a particular person's life's work is for naught? Perhaps, then, his or her work has no value; or maybe the point, if not to solve an equation, is to take inventory of possibilities. Or better yet, speculate how today's actions might influence a yet unviewed documentary—what if we could anticipate the fast forward? You're still on the couch with your red, swollen ankle elevated on a tower of throw pillows; if you knew the convulsions would lead to paralysis, would you still hesitate to reach for the phone?

I imagine myself in this situation, pondering, hesitating. Who would I call? My father, perhaps.

When we returned from each desert trip, my father meticulously labeled each jar, either by placing a handwritten note inside or by taping a typewritten note to the outside.

```
Paruroctonus silvestrii: Las Estacas, Mexico--
1971
Family Vejovidae--it stings but is not fatal.
B. Firstman
```

At the height of his career he'd amassed at least a thousand jars, each containing from one to a dozen arachnid specimens. Inside transparent, circular tombs, each creature drifted in a sort of limbo—neither alive nor allowed to begin the process of decomposition that would make them part of the soil, contributing to the next cycle of life. Upon retirement, my father gave most of them to colleagues. Today only a few jars remain.

When he calls again to add more things to his list, I do not tell him I've taken his scorpion, the one that, for reasons unknown to me, he deemed worthy of saving. It floats in suspended animation just an arm's reach from my desk.

"And my electric typewriter," he says. "And ribbon cartridges. All of them."

"Yes, I already packed those."

"You'll find them in my bottom desk drawer."

"Already got 'em."

"Pull the drawer fully open and look behind the metal divider."

"Uh-huh," I say, because I know he cannot stop. I reach for the scorpion and hold it eye level. Much of the formaldehyde has either leaked or evaporated.

"Are you writing all this down?"

"Yes, of course," I say, and I wonder if the amount of liquid affects the preservation of the dead animal, if I should remove the cap and add more liquid. It would be a shame, after all these years, to let this particular scorpion dry up and crumble.

PART II

Scorpions, Snakes

Twelve

Visalia, California (2013)—

I recall a certain photo.

When I was a young child, maybe three or four years old, I pulled my mother's bra from a basket of clean laundry and put it on. I remember standing in my underpants with the bra straps hanging from my bare shoulders, then calling out for someone to come see what I'd done. My mother ran into the room, told me not to move a muscle, and disappeared down the hall again. In a few seconds she returned, with my father this time. And a camera.

I just stumbled across that photo the other day. I hardly recognize myself as the potbellied little girl in that picture; it's hard to believe that the twenty-two-ish young woman with shoulder-length hair and cat-eye glasses is my mother. Yes, I recognize our faces, but it's hard to believe how quickly time has passed.

This evening I will visit my elderly mother in the assisted living place I just moved her to. I will tuck a pillow beneath her feeble legs, adjust her mechanized recliner so she can see the small table at her side, and we will resume our current project of transferring old photographs from a disintegrating album into a new, acid-free album. My mother's neurologist says the photo album project is good cognitive therapy—it prompts her to speak, which helps with the aphasia, and it exercises her memory as well. Even if she can't recall an event right away, perhaps a photo will tickle some remote crevice in her brain, stimulate a whisper of curiosity, motivate her to search for and pry open the sealed file folders in her prefrontal lobes. She can't remember what she had for lunch an hour ago, but she can tell me all about what happened on a particular day forty-four years ago, when she and my father found me next to the laundry bin with a bra draped across my naked chest.

I was talking to a friend recently about the declining health of our parents and our increasing and ever-shifting responsibilities as adult children. As we reverse roles with our elderly parents, each party must inhabit a liminal space, the transitional terrain between past and future. For the aged parent, it's a step toward the threshold separating life and death; for the middle-aged child, it's a time for reconciliation, to settle on new terms of engagement—*You raised me, now I'll take care of you.*

I keep telling myself that if I had been raised by June and Ward Cleaver my transition would be less difficult. Obviously, my father was no Ward Cleaver, but my mother was no June, either. I imagine that if I'd had a Beaver Cleaver childhood (if I'd been Beaver's unrealized twin sister, Betty) I'd be so indebted to both my doting parents—for their constant love and support, for the fatherly advice over home-cooked meals, for their concern over my general well-being and their occasional intervention in regard to my grades, my friends, my social faux pas—that I'd happily accept my new responsibilities. I'd never complain about taking my mother to physical therapy or the fact that she resists all my attempts to help her regain bits of her independence. And as for Old Man Ward, I'd embrace him with every grateful fiber of my being, tend every aspect of his growing needs. With a smile on my face I'd drive him to every doctor's appointment, nurse him back to health after every surgery, manage his finances, buy his groceries, shuttle him to astronomy night at the senior center every Tuesday, walk five doors down the street each afternoon for a glass of iced tea. That's how I imagine it. But I'm not Beaver (or Betty). I wasn't raised by June and Ward. The Cleaver family does not exist, never did—not for you, not for me, not ever.

What is real, though, for real people grappling with real lives, is a spectrum of emotional reconciliation. This spectrum doesn't measure *what* the adult child does or how thoroughly the child cares for the aged parent in terms of tasks carried out; rather, it indicates the degree of enthusiasm or resentment the adult child feels about the situation. At one end of the spectrum, the adult child eagerly cares for the aged parent, and at the other end, bitterness, perhaps grief. *You didn't raise me one iota, dear father, so why must I take care of you now?* I'm not sure where on the spectrum I stand.

But I am certain of this: things are shifting. A few years ago my once-estranged father moved across the state and into my neighborhood so I could look after him; although he's living in Mexico for the time being, he still owns his home down the street from me—and if he were to return (and he very well might), he would again become my responsibility. After he moved to Mexico, my mother suffered a massive stroke. Her illness triggered a series of other catastrophic health complications, all unexpected, all life-engulfing; she's now an invalid who resists rehabilitation, and I'm her caregiver, responsible for practically every aspect of her life— all things logistical, medical, financial and social. Over the last year my mother has been my full-time job, and even though she no longer lives with me, since I moved her into the assisted living facility a month ago, I am overwhelmed with responsibilities I had never before fathomed.

(There's a cruel sort of irony in my mom's involuntary absence now and my father's choice to be absent for most of my life. I need you to know that although my mother and I often didn't get along while I was growing up, at least she was there, if not emotionally, at least physically. She didn't seem to enjoy being a parent, but at least she provided the basics. I want you to know that even though this book is mostly about my relationship with my father, my mother did raise my brother and me—she put in her time, worked pretty damn hard to provide a stable life for us. My point is this: I recognize the literary injustice here, how the absent parent—my father—gets the most page time.)

But here I am, middle-aged and steeped in the newfound responsibilities that come with having elderly parents. As I try to reconcile my resentment with my sense of duty, I find myself examining the nature of my relationship with each parent. *Why is this so difficult?* I ask myself over and over, and, *If I were a better person, if I weren't such a self-centered ingrate, would this transition be easier?* I wonder if there is an intellectual or psychological shift I can make, a way I can enlighten my own thinking process so that I can consciously shape and settle into my evolving role more gracefully. If I change the lens through which I view my parents, myself, our respective situations, our collective situation, will I be better able to cope with these changes? And by extension, could I then help them with their transitions, too?

Child to adult.

Adult back to child.

Life to death.

Sometimes, in my more dramatic moments, I feel like I've just stepped into the mouth of a dark cave: blinding sunlight to my right, utter blackness to my left; I lean into the grey zone, where granite stone walls shadow the shifting rocks beneath my feet. *Where do I stand?*

Perhaps I shouldn't take my position or myself so seriously. The little girl in the photo, the me wearing her mother's bra, felt no sense of obligation—she lived in the moment, in that sliver of time captured on film, the time between the opening and closing of the aperture, right before the click. Presence: when time stands independent of past or future; a moment captured on film; an ever-shifting point on the continuum of existence; what liquid prolongs for a pickled scorpion, still moist; where curiosity leads; a grain of sand so fine, so small, it settles, sinks beneath your feet unnoticed, unheard.

Thirteen

Cataviña, Mexico (1994)—

The problem with sidewinder rattlesnakes, I came to realize during a hike with my father in the Mexican desert a number of years back, is that they often bury themselves beneath the loose sand, making them difficult to spot—and easy to accidentally step on. Had I known beforehand that the sands were infested with snakes, I probably wouldn't have gone on the hike in the first place. But we'd already walked about half an hour beyond the end of the dirt road where we'd parked the car, and past the point where the gravel-crusted hardpan had gradually disappeared beneath deep shifts of fine-grain sand, when my father paused mid-stride, his brown leather boots ankle-deep in the sand, and said, rather off-handedly, "Oh, by the way, one must be careful of sidewinders."

At first I thought he joking. "You never said anything about snakes," I said.

"You probably should have worn long pants," he said.

He wore Levis, which rode high above his waist due to the clamp-on elastic suspenders beneath his untucked polo shirt. Low on his forehead perched a brimmed driver's cap made of tightly woven straw, the kind you might see in a 1940s black-and-white

photo. Directly overhead, the high-noon sun pounded down relentlessly, but the cap's visor cast a sliver of shadow across his
wire-framed bifocals and the crow's feet spreading from his tem-
ples. He tugged the visor down to his eyebrows, leaned deeply
forward at the waist, and with his feet anchored shoulder-width
apart, reached for a dried cactus-branch-looking thing on the
ground. He stood upright, waved the stick as if he were an or-
chestra conductor, and told me that from here on out I should
watch for S-shaped patterns in the sand, the telltale mark of a
snake's recent aboveground movement across the terrain. He
also warned me about sleeping snakes that might be buried
beneath the surface, and said that I should periodically test the
ground. He demonstrated with a stick, pricking and sweeping the
gravel near his feet several times. "Sidewinders cover themselves
to keep cool," he said, "so don't step on or near any suspicious-
looking mounds until you've checked." With that, he focused his
gaze farther out, turned his head side to side several times, and
pointed to an uneven, slightly elevated patch of sand several
yards away. "Definitely stay away from that," he said. He handed
me the stick and marched a wide berth around the mound and
the potential foe hidden beneath.

I gripped the poking stick and stepped slowly, wishing I'd worn
jeans instead of shorts. A layer of denim might prevent a snake's
fangs from puncturing the skin, I thought. I followed cautiously
behind my father, pausing to evaluate the safety of each foot place-
ment: Step right. Look around. Step left. Scan, scan, keep the eyes
moving, scan. Should I poke? Yes, poke. Poke again. Sweep. Nothing
there, thank God. Step right.

In a matter of minutes I'd fallen considerably behind. "Slow
down," I called out.

He did not answer, but continued on, knees raised high in
stride, arms swinging furiously back and forth.

When my father and I had set out on a two-week road trip with no particular destination in mind other than "somewhere" in Baja, Mexico, the purpose of our journey was to reconnect after a lifetime of spotty interaction, get to know each other as adults. We'd started with no preset itinerary other than a crinkled road-map courtesy of AAA and my father's catchphrase, *Let's play it by ear.* Midway through the trip, three hundred miles south of the American-Mexican border, he suggested a hike he'd heard about, which was rumored to lead to a remote site of minor, yet impressive, ancient cave paintings in a *respaldo* overhanging rock shelter in the middle of the desert.

To reach the trailhead: From Tijuana you take the toll highway south, which parallels the western coast for quite some distance before it veers inland and narrows to a two-lane strip down the center of a thin peninsula that straddles the Pacific Ocean and the Sea of Cortez. Nearly dead center in the middle of the peninsula, you'll cross a stretch of wasteland flats flanked by heat-gnawed mountains. As you descend, the arrow-straight road lances a forbiddingly jagged sprawl of wind-polished, building-sized boulders that perch upon one another in the center of 33,000 desolate square miles, where millions of scorpions and rattlesnakes populate a vast region nearly devoid of people. About a mile outside the 140-person town of Cataviña, you turn off the highway and follow a dirt road until it dead ends; from there, a two-mile walk drops into a boiling hot arroyo. Welcome to the middle of nowhere. Now follow the dry gulch until you locate a makeshift sign indicating where to begin your climb through and up the boulders to a high cave.

My father was a couple hundred yards ahead of me when he found the painted plywood sign. A stenciled arrow pointed away from the wide-open dry gulch and toward a maze of gigantic rock pilings. He cupped his hands around his mouth and shouted, "This way!"

I waved the stick overhead and shouted back a triumphant "Woohoo!"

This would have been a logical place for him to wait for me to catch up. But instead, he picked up his pace. He zigzagged uphill, childlike, through spindly boojum trunks and ten-foot-tall cardón cacti, then darted behind a massive mound of rocks, out of sight.

Still down in the gulch, I *s-l-o-w-l-y* followed my father's trail, vigorously scanning for suspicious mounds. I carefully matched my stride to his shallow boot-shaped divots, sunken little patches of pre-tested safety.

Then, just as I lifted my right leg, I heard it: a rustle, somewhere off to the left. I froze mid-step. I balanced for a moment on one foot, perfectly poised, one leg still raised in arched stride, knee bent. I held my breath and looked around. Every grain of sand popped with bionic clarity. Stagnant air tickled my fingertips, and the collective exhale of cactus and sage pierced the oxygen around my palms. I still don't know what made that particular sound at that particular moment. Perhaps it was a harmless kangaroo rat, or a lizard, or maybe it was indeed a snake—but after a thorough session of poking and sweeping and more poking, I ascertained that I stood in at least a four-foot snake-free circle, which included the upcoming two or three divots.

I thought about turning back. I could have called out, yelled for my father to return, then said that I couldn't possibly continue, that it was too dangerous and we should head back for the car. But no, I couldn't turn back—partly because I needed to prove myself to my father, show him the strong, adventurous daughter he'd missed out on all these years, and partly because I was too damn curious. I needed to see those cave paintings, to inhale in their vicinity, even though I knew practically nothing about them.

All I knew was that some sort of prehistoric art lay ahead, hidden in the caves high above.

What puzzles me now is that even though I learned about the rattlers fairly early into the hike, early enough to turn around, I still continued. I feel driven to account for my decision to put myself in obvious danger that day, particularly since I've had a lifelong phobia of snakes. In hindsight, I'm smitten by the link between curiosity and fear, intellectual and physical connections both innate and learned—not only how these emotions have evolved in humankind, but also how they manifest themselves in my character. I wonder if an examination of curiosity might help me locate myself on the spectrum of emotional reconciliation. How does curiosity work, and what forms does it take?

Fourteen

From a biological standpoint, humankind's sense of curiosity presents a paradox. As animals, our basic needs are pretty simple—food, water, shelter, and the ability to reproduce. But we humans tend to go above and beyond. Consider the complex world we've created for ourselves—the Internet, our marble-countered and triple-pane-windowed homes, lean-protein low-carb Stevia-sweetened diets, Captain Kirk–worthy iPhones, 355-horsepowered Chevy Tahoes—we long ago exceeded our basic needs. To a point, curiosity is beneficial. At its most extreme, though, our instinctual urge to gain extraneous, possibly irrelevant information can be dangerous.

For example, imagine an early humanoid standing outside a dark cave. For fun, let's say the humanoid is Chaka, the four-foot, hairy caveman-type character from the 1970s Saturday morning television show of my youth, *Land of the Lost*. (As a kid I'd wrap myself in a comforter and gorge on Cocoa Puffs, imagining myself one of the characters on the show, which revolved around the adventures of the Marshall family—father Rick, son Will, and daughter Holly—who, while on a rafting/camping trip, are swept down a gigantic waterfall and through a time vortex portal. The family, trapped in an alternate universe inhabited by dinosaurs and a primate-type humanoid species, takes shelter in a high bluff cave and eventually befriends one of the humanoids, the bipedal, flat-foreheaded Chaka.)

Imagine adorable little Chaka hungry and grunting and leaning his wide head into the mouth of a deep, dark, unknown cave (*not* the one inhabited by the Marshall family). He wonders if he might find something to eat. Or just wonders what he might find, period. Curiosity draws Chaka inside. Depending on the cave's geographical locale, he might be greeted by a coiled rattler, a poised scorpion, or a momma bear with her cubs.

Curiosity, then, seems to defy evolutionary theory. The most curious among us should've been killed off before getting the chance to reproduce, with that trait losing out to less deadly ones in the process of natural selection. We don't really need to solve the daily jumble, snoop inside the closed desk drawer, or explore the dark cave. And yet we do. Sometimes we are driven, unable to stop, unwilling to abandon the snake-riddled trail.

Remember the scorpion theft: *Alone in his house, I committed personal invasion. Snooping through his personal things was a way to get closer to the man I held at arm's length. Even if I had wanted to cease my search, it would have been impossible to stop. Impossible.*

And now: *I should turn back*, I thought as I stood in the Mexican desert, *but I cannot. I must see the ancient cave paintings for myself, inhale in their vicinity.*

We've long been aware of our curious nature, a trait generally revered among humans—save for that infamous period of intellectual obfuscation following the collapse of the Roman Empire: the Dark Ages. At the cusp of that shadowy era, Saint Augustine wrote in his autobiographical *Confessions* about "the disease of curiosity." He suggests that furthering one's knowledge purely for the sake of idle gawking invites evil because such aimless pleasure distracts us from exploring our theistic nature. Detailing regrets of his arrogant youth and subsequent conversion to Christianity, Augustine links curiosity to the sin of lust—as both, he claims, involve delving into things and people that should be deemed off limits.

But sustained aversion to curiosity, of course, would bring society to a full and complete halt. To oversimplify the obvious: if not for the flowering of science, literature, art, politics, and educational reform following the Dark Ages, our current lifestyle— the way we experience the world—would not exist. We'd have no Maxwell's equations of electricity and magnetism, no television, no *Land of the Lost*, no Hubble Telescope. No crumpled Automobile Club map, no road to Cataviña, *no exhalation of certainty from the center of this particular four-foot radius of snake-free sand*. One thing leads to another.

Fifteen

Curiosity leads to knowledge, an accumulation of information that supports humanistic needs, not only in a scientific, practical sense, but also on a personal, existential level. It was the latter that fueled our father-daughter, play-it-by-ear road trip to Baja in 1994, the journey that led us to the boulder fields of Cataviña. Although I was unaware of it at the time, several shades of existential curiosity came into play when we planned that trip, shades that still evolve today, full-hued and ever-changing.

"I have so many things I want to tell you," my father had said on the phone earlier that year, "about the origins of life and the universe and what it all means."

Although my interactions with my father during the preceding twenty years had been limited to two dozen or so strained phone calls and half as many month-long summertime visits to his home four hours away, some parental guidance sounded great. I was thirty at the time, and he was sixty-six. Perhaps it was my own growing maturity, or maybe it was the fact that I was in the process of a divorce, living by myself for the first time in my life, and generally struggling through a tough period—for whatever reason, I felt the need to get to know my father. Adult to adult, on equal terms.

Call it curiosity.

What a shame it would be if I never got to know him, to absorb his wisdom. I would have been happy with menial advice on how to get rid of the mouse in my kitchen, but a summation of existential reflection from a learned biology professor, a man of whom I knew so much *about* and yet so little *of?* It was a *Tuesdays with Morrie* proclamation, this universe-and-what-it-all-means offer—a gesture that promised insight as well as a very late back payment toward a longstanding parental debt.

Of course, no one has the answers to grand questions about the meaning of life, the why-are-we-here contemplations that hypnotize us as we gaze into a star-filled night sky, but I was curious to hear what my father had to say. Taking a trip would give us the occasion to talk, leisurely and in depth.

"Let's go to Mexico," he said, "like we used to when I was married to your mother. Do you remember?"

Sixteen

How could I forget the way my mother's brown hair whipped against her neck as my parents' VW camper van roared down the Baja coast? The first couple nights we'd camp on the beach and fall asleep to the ping-ping-ping of the tent's unzipped flap as it bounced against the aluminum poles, silver in the moonlight, leaning into the salt wind. Then back on the road, the highway veered inland. We raced toward distant pools of water across the road that, as we neared, morphed into waves of heat that billowed into the yellow sky. Each time my father pulled off the road he'd mop his neck with a handkerchief before stooping in the gravel with his index cards and empty glass jars.

As a child, I hadn't realized the value of my father's studying scorpions, other than the immediate benefit they served as general samples to show his students. In fact, I never gave the why-would-anyone-study-scorpions question much thought until after my thievery of his favorite specimen, the one he captured in 1971 in Las Estacas, Mexico. Since that theft, which triggered a scientific, Google-by-night-public-library-by-day curiosity, I've come to recognize the biological significance and medicinal potential of scorpions, including the recent development of venom-based pharmaceuticals that fight cancer, treat stroke patients, and prevent malaria. In deeply examining scorpions, we have extended that knowledge and applied it to ourselves. While most of us loathe wild scorpions—shriek and jump back when we find one under a rock or in the backyard—I sure was thankful for my bottles of venom-based anti-malaria pills when I went to Africa and Ecuador. (And I was just visiting, unlike the millions of people who live with the threat of this disease every day.)

But it wasn't scientific curiosity that prompted me to steal the scorpion—no, the all-night Google pursuit did not motivate my little robbery. I snagged the scorpion because I was driven by a curiosity neither scholarly nor literary, but rather personal and visceral: who is this man, my father? Perhaps I took his scorpion in an attempt to recapture the sense of adventure and security that I felt when we traveled through the desert as a family those many years ago—the bottled scorpion a talisman of an almost forgotten father-daughter connection that diminishes with each passing year, like a dream dissipating in morning's light until only an undefined emotion remains.

And I think it was a similar kind of curiosity that made the proposed road trip to Mexico so attractive. The thought of exploring the Baja Desert, of retracing the roads and the hikes we'd taken during my childhood—it all seemed so irresistible as I sat alone in my under-furnished one-bedroom apartment with the receiver pressed against my ear and the spiral phone cord wrapped around my index finger. What a gift. I could get to know my father, the parent I'd never known, not *really*. What's he like? How will it be, just him and me, alone in nature? Perhaps this trip would make up for lost time, like a cram session before a final exam proctored by Professor Grim Reaper. I was incredibly curious. What parental guidance, what father-figure wisdom, had I missed out on?

The idea of getting to know him, to relate as autonomous adults, appealed to me. Although I wasn't with him in the mid-seventies when he rolled the camper van off the Baja highway embankment (spewing hundreds of loose pages of his in-progress Stanford dissertation all over the dry roadside), I've heard the story so many times it seems like my own memory. I can see him zooming southbound from Rosarito toward San Quintín, game for anything new—music, food, language, social conventions, women, or a hit of acid while lying alone on his open-air cot, miles from the nearest rancher's house, his limbs splayed beneath the Milky Way.

His being the outsider seems to excite rather than inhibit the character I've created in my mind: a cross between a nerdy professor and an overage hippie, with shoulder-length red hair, worn leather boots tied at the ankle, and a large peace sign pendant bouncing against his sternum. As I've said, he was never what you'd call a traditional, involved father. But he was sort of a cool guy in other ways, up for any adventure, anywhere. And when the van veered full throttle off the highway in 1973 and rolled four times down the steep embankment, he miraculously crawled out the open window of the upturned vehicle and chased his papers on hand and knee, frantically slapping his palms against loose-leaf pages filled with field notes and diagrams of arachnid anatomies.

His fearlessness, his uninhibited desert explorations, and even his lead-foot approach to life—while these character traits pushed against the boundaries of others' expectations, to the point that they might qualify as personality flaws, to me they seemed proof of his invincibility. And that's what appealed to me, to the grown daughter with the receiver pressed against her ear.

On the other hand, I was motivated by something more than a nostalgic longing to recapture an idealized father-daughter bond that may never have existed in the first place. Yes, a shade of curiosity, but also fear—the fear of death, not my own but his. I couldn't have articulated it the day I sat in my apartment with the swamp cooler blowing and the receiver slipping against my sweaty cheek, but I was preparing myself for his eventual exit from this planet. His sixty-six years seemed incredibly old to me at the time. I wondered: How would I feel if he died today and I hadn't forgiven him for what I perceived as his parental shortcomings? If I didn't make peace with him while he was still alive, how would I feel when he was gone? Would I have regrets? On some level I realized I was still trapped by my inability to forgive his parental absenteeism; I was ready to begin the purging of a lifelong grudge that must precede my getting to know him as an adult. The real him, though—not the polarized still-frame images of either heroic perfection or demonic culpability (depending on the filter of my recall). And this forgiveness-in-order-to-know was not of the What-Would-Jesus-or-Buddha-or-Mohammed-Do variety; no, it sprang from neither a moralistic nor sympathetic state of mind, but rather, it emerged totally self-serving on my part. I was pre-treating my anticipated pain of his eventual death, however far off that might be, like taking two aspirin and gulping down a big glass of water before stumbling to bed after a night of heavy drinking. I sought to prevent my own existential hangover.

My father repeated his question over the phone. "How about it? Mexico, just you and me?"

"Sounds good," I said. "Where will we go, exactly?"

"Let's play it by ear."

Seventeen

Question: If I'd known ahead of time that snakes might lay hidden beneath the sand, would I have gotten out of the car in the first place? Would I still go on the hike?

Answer: Probably not.

Answer amendment: Looking back, I see that what I was looking for, what I sought, wasn't the cave paintings, per se, but adventure. So maybe I would have gone anyway. That's what the whole Mexico road trip was about. Adventure. Everybody knows that driving around Mexico is risky to begin with. Then add a snake-addled hike to the mix. Now we're talking danger. Going on an adventure—saying to yourself, "I don't know exactly what I'm getting into or what will happen, but I trust myself to navigate through the unknown"—allows you to find out what it is you don't know about yourself. Unless you push yourself into unknown territory, unless you give yourself the opportunity to assess a new situation, ask yourself a series of impromptu questions—follow my father through the snake-infested sand or head back to the car?— well, what better way to learn a little something about yourself, surprise yourself?

This principle underlies not just human psychology, but scientific inquiry as well.

Case in point: Recently, in a climate-controlled room at the University of Northern Colorado, stacks of clear-sided drawers and cluttered countertops surrounded a middle-aged, bearded man in a button-down shirt. Professor Steve Mackessy carefully lowered a long, J-shaped hook into a thick glass box containing a sprawled but very alert rattlesnake. Fluorescent lights buzzed overhead as he gently slid the hook underneath the snake and lifted it from the pen, then grasped the creature barehanded, keeping his fingers behind the animal's head. In reflex, the snake opened its mouth, revealing two fangs, each capable of delivering lethal amounts of venom. Mackessy guided the fangs over a small, wide-mouth plastic measuring cup, where drops of yellow poison fell.

Since 1994, Mackessy's research on the biology of venomous snakes and the biochemistry of those venoms has centered on the hopes of developing an anti-cancer drug. Not unlike our discoveries of the medicinal uses for scorpion venom, snake venom has a lot of potential. Toxins promise life. "The difference between drugs and poison is a matter of dosage," the inquisitive Mackessy said in a recent interview.

After extraction, the venom is frozen and stored for research. Crude venoms—venoms taken directly from the snakes—are introduced to cultured breast cancer cells to answer general questions in early-stage experiments: which types of venom kill or inhibit the growth of cancer cells? Later, more complicated tests involve breaking venoms down into smaller components in an attempt to learn what, exactly, inside each venom is useful, and how those compounds might be developed into lifesaving drugs. While Mackessy's team is far from producing any drugs yet, he thinks within the year he will have enough data to begin the next stage of in-depth research.

My point here is that scientifically motivated curiosity like Mackessy's and my father's illustrates another shade of curiosity and exemplifies our need to exceed the most basic knowledge (*Will the snake bite?*). But this is just the tip of the iceberg. While biologists have inventoried over two thousand species of venomous snakes, we know relatively little about most of them, and unless we keep asking questions, we can't know what it is we don't know. We're still too clueless to realize we haven't a clue.

"The work is just starting," Mackessy said gleefully of the research ahead, "enough to keep me busy for the rest of my life."

And that's how it is for me, too—trying to figure out my father, myself, my present position on the spectrum of reconciliation. The work is just starting, enough to keep me busy for the rest of my life. As my parents age, as my duties as an adult daughter shift, relative both to their decline and to the state and logistics of our respective relationships (Will my father continue to live in Mexico or will he return to Visalia? Will my mother move back into my spare bedroom, or will I take on an additional job to pay for a nice assisted-living facility?), I constantly navigate unknown terrain. Each phone call is a sinuous lump in the sand. Is my father calling to say he's moving back? Is the caretaker calling to say my mother's needs are too high for assisted living? For most of my adult life, I've considered my parents' well-being separate from my own: my parents are kinda crazy, I'd say, but we stay out of each other's way. Now our paths have merged. My father's and my mother's trails have veered into mine.

Question: Hypothetically speaking, had the notion of scientific or medicinal potential occurred to me out there in the boulder fields of Cataviña where I scanned the sand for suspicious-looking mounds, would I have conceded some similar potential benefits to the likes of rattlesnakes, too?

Answer: Maybe.

Answer amendment: Even so, such thoughts would not have comforted me in the moment, would not have eliminated the fight-

or-flight tingle in my palms as I balanced on one foot, listening for the *tstststststs* of sidewinders. I'm okay with the stolen formaldehyde-soaked scorpion floating in its jar inside my desk drawer (though I admit to a ting of the heebie-jeebies when I jiggle the jar back and forth to feel its forty-plus-year-old body shift limply from side to side). I'm okay with thousands of scorpions in thousands of jars, as a matter of fact, and throw in a few hundred pickled spiders as well. But snakes: no can do. Not dead, not alive, and certainly not loose and unaccounted for, poking stick or not. I fancy myself the Indiana Jones type—allow me an adventure, an impromptu hike in the desert, but please, no snakes.

Intellectually, I get it: curiosity + scientific inquiry = knowledge.

Emotionally, not so much: my palms still sweat at the thought of Indiana Jones trapped in the Well of Souls—the secret underground cave containing the Ark of the Covenant—vipers slithering around his torso, between his legs, heaving across his collarbone. I turned seventeen the summer *Raiders of the Lost Ark* debuted in 1981. I returned to the theater five times during a month-long visit to my father's house in Southern California, each time to relive Indiana's adventure vicariously, outrunning Nazis and booby traps and wrath-of-God forces. I remember the expression on Harrison Ford's face as my friend Lana and I stared up at the big screen, his wide-eyed gaping grimace as he sat momentarily paralyzed with fear in the snake hell of that dark, dangerous cave. Lana's head flinched backward as she sank lower into the cushioned seat next to mine, and I, too, crouched down involuntarily, turning my head slightly to the right as if viewing from an angle rather than straight on would somehow protect me from the serpents on screen. I remember Lana's forehead and cheeks illuminated by the screen's reflection, her expression mirroring my own: lips apart, teeth clenched together, eyebrows arched—the face of fear.

Eighteen

We all recognize this face.

We study it.

The "face of fear" became a talking point during the nineteenth-century debate surrounding Charles Darwin's theory of evolution, whereupon Darwin conducted his own experiments on facial expressions.[1] The nature of his inquiry[2] speaks to the universality of Indiana's facial expression (and is also perhaps testament to Harrison Ford's acting skills). Lana and I, along with all the other teenagers cowering in the Pomona Triplex Theater that summer afternoon, instantly identified with our hero's grimace. Our imaginations ran wild with deep-seated recognition.

---

1. Darwin believed the universal bug-eyed stretched-mouth terror was an instinctive tightening of muscles triggered by an evolved response to fear, a point he sought to prove in the reptile house of the London Zoological Gardens. Trying to remain perfectly calm, he stood as close to the glass as possible while a puff adder lunged toward him on the other side. Each time he grimaced and jumped back, then saddled up again for another go. In his diary he wrote, "My will and reason were powerless against the imagination of a danger which had never been experienced," concluding that ancient instinct still reminisces, untouched by the nuances of modern civilization.

2. I question Darwin's scientific method for this particular experiment. Really, Chuck? You're gonna "prove" what you already believe to be true by using yourself as the subject? No conflict with objectivity there.

The universal-fear concept manifests in all sorts of contemporary artistic endeavors, from movies to television to literature. Like Carl Sagan's sci-fi novel *The Dragons of Eden*.[3] Or the movie *Snakes on a Plane*. Or the giant snake in *Conan the Barbarian*. The list goes on.

Time and again modern pop culture capitalizes on the universal-fear theme. Consider television's *Fear Factor*, where for six seasons NBC offered a weekly $50,000 prize to the contestant who managed to choke down a blended rat smoothie or immerse his head in a box of live, limbless, elongated reptiles: snakes. Several years later, I still remember the lunchtime talk in the teacher's lounge back in 2006, the day after the blended rat smoothie episode. Who could forget a blended rat smoothie?[4]

Recent Gallup Polls reveal that the most common fears in American teenagers in the United States include snakes, rats, public speaking, nuclear war, being alone, going to the dentist, and heights. Ah, snakes and rats. No surprise there. Lana and I could have told you that thirty years ago. What I couldn't have told you then is that we're genetically predisposed to fear potentially poisonous, disease-carrying animals that once posed significant danger to early humans. This may account for universal phobias that span cultures and continents. It makes sense if you think about fear as an evolutionary instinct embedded in human consciousness.

---

3. The book's title derives from his thesis that the instinctual mammalian fear of reptiles is a genetic endowment left over from a titanic battle between mammals and reptiles; mammals emerged victorious, at least temporarily, in the evolutionary struggle for dominance, but the remnants of that struggle live on in our myths and subconscious fears.

4. Of course this show was popular (even if you weren't interested in the interpersonal dramas bouncing like spears between arguing and posturing reality TV cast members). We could identify with the (albeit artificially created) plight of the players. From the comfort of our La-Z-Boy recliners we indulged our voyeuristic curiosity while vicariously facing our own fears, speculating on our own ability to enter the darkened cave, touch the snake, eat the rat.

Cute little Chaka and his humanoid clan survived the dangers of nature by adapting to their environs. Sometimes Chaka got lucky, but often he was extraordinarily capable of detecting and deterring the threat of, say, a poisonous snake.

In the journal *Psychological Science*, the theory of an innate, visually stimulated fear mechanism is supported by a series of experiments comparing the abilities of adults and three-year-olds to quickly and accurately pinpoint images of snakes among harmless distractions.[5] Parents and children identified snakes more rapidly than they detected the other stimuli, despite the gap in age and experience. The study also found that both children and adults who don't fear snakes are just as good at quickly identifying them as children and adults who do fear snakes.

So perhaps Chaka's survival-serving fear hardwired itself into Indiana's genetic code before Indiana was even a glimmer in George Lucas's eye.

Perhaps my parents' personality traits—even the behaviors that drive me mad—are hardwired into my genetic code. Perhaps we're not so different, my father and I, my mother and I. Perhaps, at least partially, I resent taking care of them because in reality, behind the resentment, lies fear. Maybe I dread my own decline.

When I study that old photograph, the one with a potbellied little girl wearing her mother's bra and the twenty-something mother next to her, I see myself in my mother's face.

---

5. "We wanted to know whether preschool children, who have much less experience with natural threats than adults, would detect the presence of snakes as quickly as their parents," explains University of Virginia graduate student Vanessa LoBue. Children and their parents each viewed nine color photographs on a computer screen and were asked to find the single snake among eight flowers, frogs, or caterpillars, or, alternately, the single non-threatening item among eight snakes.

Nineteen

The whispering dread of unspecified, far-in-the-future mortality (or the existential how-will-I-feel-when-my-father-someday-dies-type fear) differs from the palm-tingling fear that snapped through my senses while I hiked the deep sanded gulch of Cataviña, the kind of fear that contorted Indiana Jones's and Lana's faces during *Raiders of the Lost Ark*. It's the latter response I question here— I wonder what happened inside my brain the moment I thought I heard a sidewinder. More to the point, what are the neurological mechanics of palm-tingling fear?

Let's say you're home alone watching *Raiders of the Lost Ark* late in the wee hours. The pitch-black night presses against the uncurtained windows. Then you see it and hear it at the same time: the front door bangs, rattles against the doorframe; the knob jiggles. Your breathing speeds up. Your heart races. Muscles tighten. *What if? What if?* Your palms tingle.

Your brain's fear response triggers automatically, setting off a chain reaction that culminates with the release of muscle-energizing chemicals. You and Chaka are now one; he's alive inside your thalamus. His hairy, bare feet kick your neural impulses into hyperdrive. Chaka wonders, *Is it a burglar, or is it the wind?* His question careens down two paths simultaneously, via the low road and the high road: the low road shoots first and asks questions later, making a beeline for the hypothalamus and activating the fight-or-flight launch sequence (safer to assume it's a burglar and have it turn out to be the wind than vice versa), while the high road takes more time and delivers a more precise interpretation of events. The longer process, the high road, looks like this:

1. When your eyes and ears sense the commotion at the door,
   a. they high-priority email the information to the thalamus, who
   b. forwards the info to the sensory cortex, where
   c. it's downloaded and interpreted for meaning.

2. The sensory cortex Google-searches,
   a. determines that there is more than one possible interpretation of the data, and
   b. passes the cumulative info along to the hippocampus, with
   c. a post-script requesting additional context.

3. The hippocampus mass-text-messages inter- and intra-department-wide questions like,
   i. "Hey, everyone, haven't I seen this particular stimulus before?"
   ii. "If so, what did it mean that time?"
   iii. "Can I get an archive search of long- and short-term memories ASAP?"
   iv. "What might give me clues as to whether this is a burglar or a wind storm?"

   b. Then the hippocampus intercepts the resulting data scurrying along the high road, such as:
      1. the tapping branches against a window,
      2. a muffled howling sound outside,
      3. and the clatter of patio furniture flying about.

   c. Taking into account this other information, the hippocampus determines that the door action is most likely the result of wind.

d. Finally, the hippocampus
    instant-messages the amygdala
    that there is no danger after all,
    1. and the amygdala in turn
    2. tells the hypothalamus to
        shut off the fight-or-flight
        response
    3. (with a cc to Chaka, who's
        poised for battle, fire poker
        raised overhead).

4. Even though the sensory data regarding
    the door runs down both paths at the
    same time, the high road takes longer
    than the low road. Hence the moment of
    terror before you calm down. That's when
    you flop to the couch in an exhalation of
    relief, put the fire poker down—and
    wonder when, exactly, you picked it up in
    the first place—then push the rewind
    button on the remote control: Ok,
    Indiana, where were we?

Twenty

Regardless of which path we're talking about—high or low road—all roads lead to the hypothalamus, which is the fight-or-flight command center of our ancient survival instincts. If we couldn't feel fear, we wouldn't survive long. Unfettered curiosity could lead us blindly through an isolated maze of hazards. We'd carelessly handle poisonous snakes, traipse the Cataviña boulder fields without a poking stick, and hang out with tuberculosis-infected coughers. So some of Chaka's humanoid friends perished before reproducing; others, those who feared the right things, survived to pass on their genes.

When it comes to fear, what doesn't kill us just might excite us—the gene-passing, DNA-mixing kind of excitement. When the hypothalamus turns on the fight-or-flight response, the sympathetic nervous system and the adreana-cortical system flood the bloodstream with dozens of hormones: the heart pounds, pupils dilate, veins constrict, glucose increases, skin prickles, certain muscles tense, others relax, oxygen intake increases, attention narrows and locks onto the object in question. The effect can be quite pleasurable, even mimic (ahem) sexual arousal. No wonder so many people see scary movies and ride roller coasters with their dates. No wonder the carnal investigation, groping teenage couples in the back rows of movie theaters or skin-to-skin explorations behind steamy car windows, hands and fingers and tongues searching in the dark.

Scientific evidence supports the fear-attraction connection. Psychologist Arthur Aron, for instance, conducted a study using the very common fear of heights. One group of men walked across a 450-foot-long, unstable-feeling bridge suspended over a 230-foot drop; another group walked across a perfectly stable-feeling bridge over the same height. At the end of each bridge, the men met Aron's very beautiful female assistant. She asked each subject a set of questions related to an imaginary study and then gave him her phone number in case he wanted more information. Of the thirty-three men who'd walked across the stable bridge, two called the assistant. Of the thirty-three who'd walked across the swaying bridge, nine called. Aron concluded that the state of fear encourages sexual attraction. Which may account for my (still-lingering) wild crush on Harrison Ford. And my personal all-time record for seeing the same movie in a single theater run. One summer, five times, full ticket price. (Many years have passed since he first played Indiana Jones in 1981, but like a good wine, the man gets better and better with age. Still.) One can only imagine the rollicking good time Chaka initiated when he returned to camp late at night after a harrowing day of dark-cave exploration and rattlesnake scares.

Curiosity, as a concept, occupies a liminal space: it teeters on both edges of the good-to-bad spectrum, pulls the opposite ends together, magnetizes their polarities until the straight-lined spectrum arches, bends into a circle, fuses, and emerges as a ring, a band without beginning or end. For better or worse, curiosity and fear cohabitate, live as one. They are the Odd Couple of human behavior, the Oscar Madison–Felix Unger, love-hate couple nesting in your brain.

For Chaka, though, it all worked out (not so for his dearly departed brother, Tuktuk, may he rest in peace). In this case, curiosity led Chaka to new food sources hidden in the dark cave; inside the cave, he grabbed the food but then had to fight off the vipers; thoroughly turned on, he went home and banged Mrs. Chaka (and probably his newly widowed sister-in-law, Mrs. Tuktuk, as well); his offspring (and their offspring and theirs) eventually emerged preprogrammed with a heightened sense of curiosity and willingness for adventure, but also a genetically based innate fear of reptiles, which enabled them to easily discern a rattler among flowers and frogs and shaded dry grass.

In this I take comfort. It is unlikely that my eight-year-old niece will want to bend over and touch the coiled rattlesnake she might discover beneath my brother's deck. Genetic programming protects the little girl that carries my parents' (and her parents') genes.

Twenty-One

From the makeshift sign, I followed my father's trail of footsteps through the sandy gulch, making good use of my poking stick. I hadn't seen him since he darted into the maze of rock pilings, but the trail soon rose out of the dangerously loose sands of the gulch and onto higher, firmer terrain. While I was still on high alert for sidewinders, fear loosened its grip on my hypothalamus and wiggled its tail in some other lobe, tantalizing my brain, tickling me with the promise of adventure, of exploration and discovery.

In a way it was like reliving the past, reenacting a version of the scorpion-collecting treks of my childhood—or just as easily, I could have inserted our faces (mine and my father's) in a *Land of the Lost* fantasy; instead of rushing through the rapids in a blow-up raft and plunging through a dinosaur-day time warp vortex like Father (and Will) and Holly did during each Saturday morning's opening credits, we trudged through Mexican desert sands and climbed the boulders in search of a certain dark cave.

As I've said, it probably wasn't the Mexican cave paintings themselves that mattered so much—what they looked like, I mean, or their shapes or intended meanings. It was the journey that mattered. And more specifically, it was the fact that this hike, this impromptu diversion from the highway, evolved spontaneously.

My father had "heard about the trail from someone," he'd said, "or else I read about it somewhere." Based on that scrap of information, we asked the locals if they knew what we were searching for, if they knew where we could find the cave paintings.

And here we were.

The sun had moved slightly to the west by the time I caught up to my father. Several more makeshift signs pointed me in the right direction through the maze of boulders, and when I arrived at the base of a particularly high piling, maybe a hundred feet tall, my father called down to me, shouting and waving his arms overhead. I climbed up with ease. At the top of the rock pile we found the *respaldo* overhang, a cave-like shelter that had been formed when a massive boulder came to rest on smaller surrounding boulders. We stepped into a shallow tunnel that was perhaps ten feet deep, six feet wide and five feet tall. The ceiling and sloping sides of the cave were covered in pictographs, overlapping images painted in red, orange, yellow, black, and white.

We sat for a long while in the shaded overhang, sipping from our canteens and gazing silently at the faded amorphous shapes stained into the granite walls. I didn't know what the pictures were supposed to represent or how to interpret them. It did appear to me, though, that this artwork had been created over a long stretch of time. Layers of images overlapped, with vivid lines—perhaps the most recent—covering bits of faded images beneath, and fainter images still beneath those. I imagine these walls had been decorated over time by many generations of indigenous kinsmen, extended family members from long-lost tribes who reigned for hundreds, perhaps thousands of years.

I tried to make sense of these tantalizing pictures. A yellow circle with black lines radiating outward: perhaps a sun. A red circle outlining a larger red circle: maybe an eclipsed moon. A cloud shape filled with dots: a rare, impending storm. A long yellow cylinder, narrowed to a point at both ends, with claw-like protrusions reaching outward from the belly: could be a scorpion. Two squiggly lines paralleling each other, trailing up the wall, wide at the bottom and narrow at the top: a path. My brain tried to assign meaning to the chaos of images, but they were impossible to interpret.

My father and I didn't talk much, at least not then. We just sort of sat. Nodded, sipped.

"I have so many things I want to tell you," my father finally said.

"Hmm?"

"About the origins of life and the universe and what it all means."

Here he picked up the thread of what had been, since the onset of this road trip several days before, his ongoing monologue about the Big Bang, the chemical composition of the sun, the diameter of Jupiter, the evolution of life on Earth, the anatomy of scorpions prehistoric and present, the loves of his life unrequited and otherwise, career accomplishments and regrets, the impossibility of God, the impossibility of a universe without God, his hope for immortality—if not via the dogma of organized religion, then how? An associative, non-linear discourse that circled around itself and repeated many times—a soliloquy I'd hear for years to come, often verbatim, other times expanded, reframed, re-imagined, re-questioned, re-answered. Curiosity pulses through my father's veins—his whole life has been a search for something more, a quest to answer his own intellectual queries, a series of questions that lead one to another, culminating with perhaps the biggest question of all: why are we here, us humans on Earth?

Isn't that the driving force behind so much of what we do? We seek answers. We want to know more. One question leads to another.

This strange motivation we humans have, to explore our world, to gain knowledge beyond what we need to survive, has taken us to the moon, expanded our mastery of internal medicine, and lent us a better understanding of our neurological functions, of our very genes. We search for our place among other humans—people living among us: father to daughter; people living epochs apart: prehistoric hunter to modern scholar. I'm drawn to these impossibilities—of understanding the world, understanding my father.

I'm still not exactly sure who sat with my father in the cave, which of my many selves sipped from the canteen. I was three people at once: part Holly, following her father in *Land of the Lost*; part Indiana Jones, swashbuckling through the snake-filled Well of Souls; and as much as I hate to admit it, part *Fear Factor* contestant, a bare-legged hiker craving a blended rat smoothie.

Herein lies a major difference between my father and myself: for him, the meaning of life might be found somewhere in absolute facts and scientific theory. For me, the answer (or at least part of the answer) might hide in the shadows cast by humans as they interact with nature and with each other. Still, I'm smitten by scientific inquiry. What fun it is to follow the circuitous path of question-leads-to-question—to reconstruct or deconstruct the making of knowledge based on observation and experimentation and quantifiable outcomes. But I'm even more interested in how the quantifiable sheds light on the unquantifiable, the human spirit. Human interaction. My own interaction with the world, with other people, my parents, myself.

When I study the personality traits my father and I share—our openness to adventure, our inquisitive minds, our fears that perhaps our personal and career accomplishments don't add up to anything that will outlive our mortal existence, our self-centered natures—perhaps I can find a place for myself on the spectrum of reconciliation that allows for our commonalities and our differences. While our individual choices and approaches to life differ, we also overlap. As I grapple with the new rules of engagement, as I take on these new adult-daughter responsibilities, obligations I simultaneously resist and surrender to (*even though you didn't take care of me one iota, dear father*), our relationship, even today, still evolves. I suspect that after he's gone, the relationship will continue to shape itself, to stretch and change from the perspective of hindsight.

So there we sat.

From inside the cave, which was very wide and shallow and not quite as dark as I'd imagined it would be, I watched the boulders' shadows stretch across the sand below. They overlapped, layers of shadows blending, morphing together in places yet remaining distinctly separate in others. Keeping pace with the sun's migration, the shadows stretched eastward and elongated so slowly that their inch-by-inch evolution was almost imperceptible. But they did move nonetheless.

PART III

Sitting-Up Mud

Twenty-Two

(2013)—

When I arrive at my mother's assisted-living apartment, she's sitting in silence with the blinds drawn. The caregivers dote on her. They would open the blinds if she would only push the button on the pendent she wears around her neck and ask, but my mother's cognitive connections, while improving at a slow, less-than-steady pace, aren't anything like they used to be, so it doesn't occur to her to let in the natural light. She's the youngest resident here. She requires a higher than average level of care—on a scale of one to four, one being independent and four being completely bedridden, she rates at level three, which sharply contrasts with her former, active and independent self.

Level three.

Life changes in an instant. One minute you're living your life— manning the Master Gardeners' booth at the farmers' market or making a cup of peach tea or helping your eight-year-old grand-daughter memorize her multiplication tables—and the next minute you're on the floor, not sure if your granddaughter heard you say she should call 911 right away, not sure if the sirens are outside your house or inside your head, not sure if those are your children gathered round you in the emergency room. You're incoherent when the Mayo Clinic–trained cardiologist whispers to your son and daughter, "Less than a one percent chance. Say your good-byes." No one survives a ruptured aortic dissection. No one has multiple strokes at once—ischemic on the right, subarachnoid hemorrhage on the left.

Sixty-seven years old.

It's not fair.

And even if you somehow survive—if you make it through a month of cardiovascular intensive care, months of sub-acute hospital care, multiple surgeries, multiple skilled nursing facilities, a summer of home healthcare in your daughter's spare room, physical therapy, occupational therapy, speech therapy, cognitive therapy— what does it mean to merely "survive" if you're no longer your full self?

There in her new assisted-living studio apartment—a dim cave equipped with a call-button chain that dangles from the wall next to her motorized recliner, and an additional call-button pendent she wears like a necklace— my mother reaps the paltry rewards of her yearlong struggle that began a few minutes before that 911 call. Partly aware, partly not. Somewhat mobile, mostly not. Left side neglect; paralysis on one side—leg, arm, visual impairment. Chicken arm. Torso leaning, hunched chronically to the right. Weak as a baby bird. Flat affect. Chronic pain. Confusion. Short-term memory shot. Long-term memory spotty. Helpless, defiant, apathetic. Technically alive but sort of not.

To be in limbo is to inhabit an intermediate, ambivalent zone.

Level three.

Twenty-Three

I suppose my father and Stephen J. Gould are right. In the whole scheme of things, we're damn lucky to be alive in the first place.

You had a one in a googolplex chance of being here.

I'm grateful for that, to be alive. The world is a wonderful place. Relative to the universe's timeline, though, our lifespan is but a blip. A blip framed by…what? Nothingness? Darkness? Unaware, pure-matter existence? The universe is a swirling mass of atoms forming clumps of various things and then dissolving. Most of those atoms don't get to be alive at all. Most of those atoms don't get to be a person, fall in love, see sunsets, eat ice cream and ride bikes, feel the ground shake when the continent shifts.

Lean. Let up. Lean.

You and I are extraordinarily lucky to be one of the select, fortunate few. Kurt Vonnegut conveyed a certain kind of gratitude in his book, *Cat's Cradle,* in a deathbed confessional prayer expressed by one of his characters:

> God made mud.
> God got lonesome.
> So God said to some of the mud, "Sit up."

"See all I've made," said God. "The hills, the sea, the sky, the stars."

And I, with some of the mud, had got to sit up and look around.

Lucky me, lucky mud.

I, mud, sat up and saw what a nice job God had done.

Nice going, God!

Nobody but you could have done it, God! I certainly couldn't have.

I feel very unimportant compared to You.

The only way I can feel the least bit important is to think of all the mud that didn't even get to sit up and look around.

I got so much, and most mud got so little.

Thank you for the honor.

Now mud lies down again and goes to sleep.

What memories for mud to have!

What interesting other kinds of sitting-up mud I met!

I loved everything I saw.

I think what Vonnegut means is that whatever the content of your life, the fact that at least you've been able to live at all is something in itself. Most mud isn't lucky enough to sit up. We're the sitting-up mud, you and I.

You had a one in a googolplex chance of being here today.

I guess the question is, then: how should we live, knowing that we're a statistical long shot and we're going to die? My immediate response is that perhaps we should be careful. Live cautiously.

Many years back, my mom and I would sometimes watch *Hill Street Blues*, a television cop show that began every episode with the sergeant summing up the various crimes and investigations that would play out in the day's program. As he sent his men out to fight crime on the streets, he'd always end by saying, "Be careful out there."

But the particular kind of care I have in mind isn't this logistical type of fact-based caution, where if you're not careful, you won't notice the big truck barreling down the street and you'll get hit and killed; or if you walk through the desert carelessly, you'll get bitten by a rattlesnake.

I stood in at least a four-foot snake-free radius, which included the upcoming two or three divots. I thought about turning back.

The fact that we're going to die seems intuitively to require a particular kind of care, because, to state the obvious, hey—you only go around once, right? The fact that we've got a finite lifespan requires us to face the fact that we could blow it. We could do it wrong. Sure, we might get some do-overs. If you live to be eighty years old, you have the chance to reappraise your life at, say, the age of thirty or forty or fifty, choose a new path. Buy a red sports car or donate all your worldly goods to charity. Or connect with your estranged daughter by taking a road trip to Baja, hike through the desert in search of ancient cave paintings. But knowing we'll die pushes us in the direction of thinking we've got to be very careful because we only have a limited period of time for those do-overs.

The way I see it, there are two kinds of mistakes we could make.

On one hand, we might discover that we've made bad choices in terms of what we were aiming for. What if my father had stayed in Pomona to read children's books aloud to me on the couch rather than driving twenty-five hundred miles cross-country to present his research to Harvard medical students?

On the other hand, we might find that even if we made the right choices in terms of our goals, we dropped the ball in terms of actually accomplishing what it is we were trying to accomplish. *Dear Rolf, I'm 48 and still alive and nobody.*

What I mean is that we have to be careful in our aims and we have to be careful in the execution of our aims. Death forces us to be careful. Yes, we've got the chance for do-overs, but we don't have time for a whole lot of do-overs.

Twenty-Four

Visalia, California (2012)—

A team of ER doctors and nurses scurried around us. They prepped my mom for surgery as we gathered round to say our goodbyes. She'd probably die any minute, one of the doctors had whispered to us in the hallway. Once the aorta burst, and it surely would, she'd be gone in three to ten seconds. "We don't expect her to make it to the operating room, but we'll prep her anyway— because, well, because it's the right thing to do," he said.

The social worker holding my hand interjected: Dr. C happens to specialize in this. He's the number-one doctor in all of California in his particular specialty.

"Get in there now," Dr. C said to us. "Hold her hand. Tell her you love her. This is your last chance. And if she doesn't go unconscious before we wheel her out, just keep talking. Talk while you can."

My brother and I must have been in some sort of stupor for them to give us such explicit instructions. I imagine we stood frozen, looking like we needed a push, a verbal list of what to do, caught in the transitional moment between hearing the information and understanding what it meant. The social worker let go

of my hand and placed her palm on my shoulder, physically guid-
ing us back into the room where my mother lay naked, her entire
torso, collarbone to hips, slathered in brown liquid. She appeared
to be covered in thin, translucent mud.

My mother's best friend was with us by now, and my husband,
too. My brother and I held her hands while the nurses inserted
catheters all up and down her arms.

But what do you say when you say goodbye?

How do you say goodbye without letting the person think
that they are *supposed* to die now, that they shouldn't keep fighting that internal battle that could make a difference, ignite
some sort of willpower that would enable them to miraculously
survive? Among other things, I decided to talk about memo-
rable events—good times, cherished memories. At first it was
easy to name and describe a few good times. But to be honest,
my mother and I have always had a somewhat contentious relationship. As a teenager and young adult, it seems like all we did
was either fight or avoid each other. When I was twenty-nine,
we went a whole year without speaking. But then, sometime
after my thirtieth birthday, we made amends—tacitly agreed it
was time for a do-over—and eventually learned to work around
each other's quirks.

My mother's body seemed to shrink as we leaned toward her
to speak, to touch her fingers. We leaned back when the nurse
reached and poked, then we drew into her again. *Lean. Let up. Lean.*
Over and over. All the while we talked, careful to speak in the present tense: You *are* a great mom; We *have* a great life together; Like,
remember the time…. And the time….

By now my brother had Googled "aortic dissection" on my
husband's phone, which we passed silently between us. The cause
of Lucille Ball and John Ritter's sudden deaths.

Talk while you can.

Three seconds turned to ten seconds. Then one minute, then five, then ten.

I struggled to keep talking.

Because, really, after "I love you" and all the obvious declarations that pour out of your mouth during the first few minutes, what else do you say when you say goodbye—when you get an unspecified amount of overtime? A deathbed do-over?

I paused to think. Memories? Memories. I needed more memories. In reality, I probably only paused for a split-nano-fraction of a second. But everything moved in slow motion, so it seemed like a long pause. A long silence. The silence stretched like a balloon, over-inflated and thin, spreading asymmetrically between past and present.

Then, click. The trip to Ecuador my mom and I had taken many years back, where we'd gone to the Amazon and the Galapagos Islands. The trip was amazing, but miserable, too. My mother and I didn't get along too well during that month-long trip, and she and I both got so sick we needed a doctor's care while traveling. My mother hated the entire trip—she discovered that she wasn't cut out for international travel, at least not in a developing country. I, on the other hand, found a new sense of freedom, a sense of empowerment that would later lead me to travel to all sorts of places, all over the world. But it wasn't the fact that I loved the trip, or that she didn't, that made me talk about it there in the surgery prep room. If my mother only had a few seconds left to live, I wanted her to remember what an adventure we had shared. How it had changed my life for the better. How I wouldn't have become who I am had she not invited me to go in the first place. So I talked. About the Galapagos Islands. The iguanas, the shark—remember that shark?—the small sailboat that carried us seven hundred miles from the shore. I talked about the Amazon. The jungle, the piranhas—remember the piranhas?—the brown water we drank each day, still slightly muddy even after being filtered. Mud every-where—remember the rubber Wellies, our legs covered in mud from the knee down each day? Remember?

We talked of other memories, too. My brother and I growing up. The grandchildren. You *are* the best mom, the best grandma. We *are* so lucky to have you. Present tense.

Draw strength from the past, but stay in the present. Lean into, inhabit the space where time sits up, independent of past or future.

My mother's eyes remained closed as we continued our good-byes—without ever actually saying the word "goodbye"—but rather, "Remember us while you're in surgery. These memories will give you strength. You'll go to sleep in a minute, and when you wake up in post-op, you'll be transformed. No more pain. Every-thing will be better."

She doesn't remember any of that now—she has no recollec-tion of the medical event, the ER, of us that night. But I believe part of her brain heard what we said, was awake and active dur-ing that liminal phase, that in-between place where her existence teetered on the threshold between life and death.

Twenty-Five

(2013)—

I push open the blinds in my mother's room so she can see the garden outside her sliding-glass door. Sitting upright in her brown mechanized recliner, she complains that the peach tea I give her is too hot and tells me to add some cold water.

"What have you done today?" I ask.

"Sit here," she says.

"What else?"

"That's it."

I ask if she's looked at the new books I left for her, if she had the caregiver wheel her to morning exercise class, if she's watched TV, if she's written (scribbled, in her case) in the notebook I left on her table.

No, no, no, and no.

"So you watched the paint peel off the walls, then?"

"Pretty much."

The room brightens even more once I turn on all the lights. Instead of a dank cave, it now feels like an inner extension of the garden outside—cheery, cozy, and colorfully decorated with Tibetan prayer flags and Eastern Indian tapestries, framed photos, her own paintings, and pink twinkly lights strung over the sliding-glass door. I ask my mother which activity we should do today. We could work on the photo album—I brought Ecuador photos—or I could read aloud, or we could watch *Monk* or *Raiders of the Lost Ark*.

She doesn't answer the question. "I've been thinking about the stupidest things all day," she says. "While I watched the paint peel."

Ah, humor. Her brain is healing. I savor each nuance like this, any sign of cognitive improvement.

My mother says she's been thinking about her childhood, and about her life with my father during the ten years they were married (the first time), and how she can't believe she put up with his behavior, especially back when they were newlyweds.

Her prefrontal lobes are waking up.

She recounts stories I already know—about the tent in the backyard, about the girlfriends who moved in with us—but I listen intently and ask lots of questions because it's good for her to talk. Cognitively therapeutic.

"My brain must have atrophied when I was a kid. When I lived in Arkansas," she says of her traumatic teenage years. "Because otherwise, why did I put up with your father?"

So instead of watching *Monk* or transferring photographs, I listen to my mother recount various episodes in her life, about how in hindsight she wishes she would have done some things differently, and how other choices she's grateful for.

"The Amazon?" I ask.

"I didn't like it."

"No?"

"But I loved it," she says. "I'm glad we went. Somewhere I saved the magazine article you wrote. Find it at my house."

"It's here in the box. An essay, though, not an article." I'm compelled to correct her, as the terms are nuanced, significant to me. Yes, my first published travel essay. Not an article—just the facts, ma'am—but an actual essay. A new beginning for me, a do-over—from third-grade teacher and moonlighting stringer newspaper reporter to literary writer. A transition from one career to the next.

"Let me see." She holds the open magazine in her lap but does not read the words. She sits in silence. She's thinking, lost in thought. Today begins what will be my mother's ongoing recall of isolated events—sporadic, unexpected slivers of time during the next several weeks where she flits momentarily from one memory to the next, relating snippets of her life, of my life, in no particular order, neither chronological nor discernibly associative. Random memories in random order. Articulated, reanimated, in sparse detail. But at least that's something. For now, though, she just gazes at the wall and rests her one good hand on the open the magazine for less than a minute. "Okay."

"Okay what?" I know what.

"I'm done."

"So what do you want?" I know what she wants. But I make her tell me in words.

"Put it away."

A bird flutters briefly outside the sliding door. It rests for a moment on the bistro table next to the hedge, then darts back up to the white sky again, disappearing.

Twenty-Six

Amazon River, Ecuador (1997)—

I was swimming alone, deep in the Amazon jungle. Pure bliss. The deep, black water of Laguna El Pilche was a cool, refreshing respite from the unrelenting humidity of the rainforest. I was treading water in the center of a muddy lagoon, about fifty feet from a swampy bank where countless water lilies, ferns, and orchids sprouted in thick masses. In the distance I could see the thatched roof of Sacha Lodge, a group of huts I'd called home for the past several days. The huts were empty. I glided farther toward the middle of the lagoon, turned onto my back, and closed my eyes. Floating belly up with my ears submerged, I heard the distinctive roar of approaching howler monkeys, their treetop cries rolling through the canopy like far-off thunder. Ah, the beauty of untamed nature.

beau•ty: The quality present in a thing or person that gives intense pleasure or deep satisfaction to the mind.

na•ture: It's my nature to define things. There's something soothing about the organized, categorized labeling of things and concepts, a shorthand to and for myself.

def•i•ni•tion: It's difficult to define my experience in the river. There's the sheer adventure of it, of course. And then there's all the backstory that leads up to the moment of clarification, the contextualized mother-daughter interactions of the past that eventually rise to the surface. Perhaps words like "parent" and "child" are impossible to define.

I'd been informed by the locals a few days before that the piranhas in these waters didn't bother people, so it was safe to swim. "As long as you're not bleeding profusely, like from an artery," I'd been told by an English-speaking guide, a young Australian woman with pointy red hair and an accent like Crocodile Dundee. "The piranhas stay down at the bottom, where it's cold and dark. Feel free to swim—all the locals do it."

So there I was. Swimming. Alone. In the Amazon. Thinking about…piranhas?

I'd read about various water-lurking creepy crawlies of the Amazon: Electric eels that produce shocks of six hundred volts; stingrays that deliver a crippling sting; and the tiny candiru catfish that can swim up the human urethra and become lodged there by implanting its sharp spines. Of course, we've all heard of the dreaded piranha. The name piranha literally means "devilfish" in Tupi, the indigenous language of this region. Little devils with razor-sharp teeth and an aggressive appetite for live meat. Sometimes human meat. A large school of these carnivorous fish were reportedly responsible for the deaths of some three hundred people several years back when their boat capsized in the Amazon River—but that was in Óbidos, Brazil, miles and miles from here. How many miles? My edition of Lonely Planet didn't say.

death: the total and permanent cessation of all vital functions; accompanied by a bright light, and then what?

And what about the animals I'd seen myself, just hours or days before? The anacondas—one of the largest species of snakes in the world, known to occasionally attack fishermen. I'd spotted them curled in the trees the previous day, and I'd read that they often lurk just beneath the water, with only their nostrils poking above the surface. And the caiman—a species of alligator that floats silently down the river at night. I was pretty sure one slept beneath my hut during the day.

From my floating position in the middle of the lagoon, my eyes jolted open and my head snapped upright. Why aren't the locals swimming today, I wondered.

Was there something I should have known? Perhaps it was a piranha-alert day, a safety warning system I didn't know about, like the tornado watches of the Midwest or the smog alerts of California.

Piranha Alert Day.

Perhaps I haven't made the best choice, I thought.

The huts, the boardwalk, the marshy bank—they were a million miles away. A mild panic rose in my chest, but I managed to swallow the fear and keep my wits. Inside me, the panic cowered inside a little box the size of a ring box—I knew that if I cracked the lid just a smidgen, it would overrun me.

Keep it down, I thought. The lid is on. On.

I sidestroked toward the dock, kicking hard and keeping my head upright.

Ears above water, I said to myself. Lid still on. What's a girl like me doing in a place like this? A girly girl. In a place like this? Lid on. Ears above. A girl like me.

I've always been a girly girl. As a child, I idolized both Farrah Faw-cett (who played Jill Munroe in *Charlie's Angels*) and Lynda Carter (former Miss World 1972, who starred in *Wonder Woman*). Thursday nights found me glued to the thirteen-inch Zenith television in our family's living room. I marveled at Linda Carter's ability to deflect speeding bullets with a flick of the wrist and a few gold bangle bracelets. And when Farrah would capture the bad guys at the end of a harrowing chase and pull a tiny weapon from her stylish high-heeled boot, I, too, would extend my arms, clasp my hands together, and stare down the barrel of my double-finger imaginary gun. "Freeze, sucker!" Farrah and I shouted in unison, our heads tilted, long blond hair spilling over one shoulder.

> **tel•e•vi•sion**: As a teenager, I spent an inordinate amount of time in my room with the door closed. The TV kept me company. I plugged it into the hot switch so that whenever I entered the room and switched the light on, the TV blinked to life.

> **i•con**: I didn't watch the Farrah Fawcett special on TV when she had cancer. To see her suffer, *anyone* suffer from cancer—I can't do it. Maybe it's the American I-can-do-anything attitude I've been steeped in, but I intensely believe (even when I know it's not rational) that we are what we think, and that a positive attitude can banish any disease. I could never admit this to anyone, but part of me actually believes that only losers die of cancer. A flawed, illogical belief, I know. It stems from my neurotic need for control.

I remember my mother's protests. "Turn that off," she'd shout at the television. As a microbiologist and college professor, she had no appreciation for perfectly coifed women who flailed about in sequined corsets and blindly took orders from a faceless man on the telephone. "We're so much more than...that," she would silently imply with a sharp glare and dismissive head shake, then flip the dial to *Mutual of Omaha's Wild Kingdom*.

"*Wild Kingdom*?" I'd cry.

"That or nothing. How 'bout nothing?"

"Might as well read the freakin' dictionary. So boring," I'd say.

"Fine." She'd push the button and the screen went black. "Then it's nothing. Enjoy the dictionary."

Just to be spiteful, to prove my point, I'd grab the paperback Webster's, plop myself down on the couch with the deepest sigh I could muster, and proceed to read. Fake reading, really, just to prove a point. To save face. *I'm reading the dictionary because I choose to, not because I lost this battle*, I glared across the room.

bat•tles: Things we had. An act of separation, even when one longs for closeness. Even when one doesn't realize one longs for said closeness.

Secretly, though, I enjoyed *Wild Kingdom*. I dreamed of venturing into the bush, standing inside zoologist Marlin Perkins's open jeep. I imagined myself the cameraperson, wheeling into the Amazon, the theme song magically emanating from an amber sky: "Mutual of Omaha: we're people you can count on when the going's rough." As the music faded, I'd wrestle an angry boa constrictor with one arm, steady the camera with the other. The snake would wrap itself around my neck, but I'd manage to free myself from its grip just in time. Gasping for breath, I'd sweep the camera back again for a panoramic view of the jungle marsh, the defeated serpent vanishing into the river.

Twenty-Seven

So when my mother invited me, Miss Girly Girl All Grown Up, to join her and her backpack-totin', Ph.D.-holdin', super-cool women friends to tromp through the ancient pyramids of South America and float down the Amazon River, how could I say no? "Count me in!" I said, because I am so much more than puffy hair and color-coordinated outfits. And thus began our five-week mother-daughter trek.

Me: the inexperienced tenderfoot, with five strong, globetrotting women. It was my chance to fit in, to prove myself to my mother. So cool, so tough, so independent.

Me: hiking boots; quick-dry cargo pants with legs that zip off to make shorts (practical, yet stylish); and a khaki safari vest with a million snap-shut, zipper-lock pouches. Because I was eager to prove my backpack-tourism toughness to the group early on, I'd even fashioned a hook that allowed my Swiss Army knife to dangle boldly from my outer vest pocket (the breast pocket where I secretly kept my lip gloss and mascara), like a bright red talisman of go-get-'em, hear-me-roar spirit. I secretly fancied myself a Charlie's Angel turned Rambo.

———

We'd been traveling nonstop for a month prior to our descent into the Amazon—through the mountains, along the coast, through villages and cities and every ancient burial ground in between. I was exhausted. I looked forward to our next stop: Sacha Lodge, set deep in the rainforest of the Upper Amazon River. I could relax, nap, and just take it easy for a few days. How much activity could there be in the jungle, after all?

> **stress**: The physical pressure, pull, or other force exerted on one thing by another; strain; what I caused my mother; what my mother inflicted upon me. Past, present, and future.

> **trau•ma**: Just being with my mother causes me trauma. We have an odd energy together, strained. *Why am I here? Remember the battles? I should have stayed home.*

Getting to the lodge turned out to be an adventure in itself. From high in the Andes Mountains of central Ecuador, we took a forty-five-minute plane ride from the bustling megacity of Quito to the remote port town of El Coca. Before boarding a twelve-passenger plane, we each stepped on a scale—our seat assignments were determined by the scale's readout, so as to distribute our collective weight evenly. "You on the right," the copilot instructed with a wave of his arm as we stepped into the plane, "and you on the left." I sat in front, right behind the pilot. My mother sat one row back on the left. While we seemed to be polar opposites, Dr. Rambo Microbiologist vs. Miss Glitter Lips, we apparently balanced each other out.

Once we were in the air, the copilot also acted as our flight attendant. He turned from his seat in the cockpit, stood before me, and filled a platter with packages of crackers and small bottles of juice. "Take one and pass it back," he announced in broken

English as he handed me the goods. "And the last person please send the plate forward again."

I heard the crinkle of cellophane behind me and I knew my mother was filling her fanny pack with Saltines. Always preparing. Rambo in action. When the cracker basket came back my way again, I purposefully did not take any more—out of stubborn habit, I suppose—simply because my mother had.

It was a bumpy ride over the Eastern Andes, and the turbulence made drinking juice through a straw almost impossible, if not comical. I suspect the pilots were secretly amused. Stupid Americanos.

While in an airplane, it's best not to think about the possibility of a crash, at least that's my theory. Like not thinking about cancer. Or a heart attack. Or stroke. If you don't give it mental energy, it's not as likely to happen. Crashing is for losers.

So while I tried not to think about crashing into the Andes' snow-covered peaks, I accidentally did think about crashing, which made me think of Linda Carter and Farrah Fawcett. Who would be more likely to survive a fiery plane crash—Wonder Woman or Charlie's Angel? Wonder Woman would definitely have the edge, what with her superpowers. She'd probably somersault out the open door of the plane as it plunged downward. *The engine coughs and sputters toward the mountainside, flames shooting along the underside of the wings. And just as the plane pierces the mountain nose first, Wonder Woman lands squarely on her feet a safe distance away from the explosion.* Yes, Wonder Woman would have the advantage. Farrah would still be in her seat, braced for impact with her head between her knees, buried in the carnage of metal and plastic and foam seat cushions melting in a ball of fire. Melting in the snow. Farrah would melt.

She was only on the show for one full season, along with six guest appearances during later seasons. Funny how we equate her with the other angels, since she probably had the shortest stint, much shorter than Kate Jackson. Kate was the smart one, sensible and serious. But we remember Farrah. She jiggled and bounced as she ran through the city's back alleys in leopard-print slingbacks. Barbie-like. Sort of dumb, with that gigglish laugh, but graceful in a shallow sort of way. She always came through, though; the bad guys never got away. Decades after the show, when her career was in the dumps, she rolled her naked body all over a huge canvas, smearing herself in paint. It sold for tens of thousands of dollars, I think. She was actually an accomplished sculptor, made a large collection of pieces. And just a few years ago she appeared on David Letterman, so vacuous and distracted that everyone thought she was high, including Letterman. I don't think so. It was a publicity move. She was relying on her old parlor tricks, the I'm-dumb-and-cute shtick. It failed. I guess we expected more from her. We expected that she'd have grown up.

No, Farrah. You're so much more than...*that*, I thought, as I pushed "off" on the remote control.

Twenty-Eight

Once on the ground, we piled our bags and ourselves into the back of a flatbed truck for a ride across town. The hot, humid atmosphere in El Coca was quite a shock after the chilly altitude of Quito. But even more of a shock were the oil-covered black dirt roads and the all-pervasive evidence of the oil industry. It made me ashamed of my car back home, of my car-dependent lifestyle. I felt shallow, self-centered, the me-centric American. The me who watches television and drives to the mall to buy makeup and clothes, the me who can afford preventive health care and adventure vacations to underdeveloped countries, the me who spent ten times more money on round-ticket airfare from Los Angeles to Quito than a family in El Coca makes in a year.

The flatbed delivered us to the bank of the muddy Napo River, one of the Amazon's one thousand tributaries. From there we took a three-hour trip in a covered, motorized canoe. It rained furiously all the while. Although the Napo is half a mile wide in some places, it is often surprisingly shallow. Since pushing a large canoe full of people off a sandbar was not something the crew wanted to do, we zigzagged down the river following the deepest channels, avoiding trees that had fallen in recent floods.

We passed many indigenous Quichua communities situated along the riverbanks, where small, thatched-roof houses stood on stilts and children played in *chacras*, small gardens growing coffee, bananas, and yucca. Mommas chasing babies with other babies strapped on their backs.

There's a bond that my mother and I share. We're so different and we often don't get along, but she'll always be my mom. A month before we left for Ecuador, she bought me a Lonely Planet book and a Spanish-English phrasebook. "There's a dictionary in the back," she said as I thumbed through the Getting Around and Shopping sections of the phrasebook. "You can look up a word in either language."

"River," I read. "Rio. Thanks."

Somewhere deep in the jungle (had the driver-guide not spoken English, I'd have been sure we were hopelessly lost, never to be found), we left our motorized boat and walked along a slippery village path that led to an elevated boardwalk through a flooded palm forest.

My mother stopped and pointed. Two giant electric-blue butterflies clung to huge leaves overhead. "It's an omen," she said.

"Yes, a good one," I said. I took out my phrasebook and turned to the dictionary. "Butterfly: mariposa. Blue: azul." That's when it dawned on me that we weren't so different, my mother and I. There we were, in a strange land far from home, carrying slightly different items—lip gloss in my pack, Pepto-Bismol tablets in hers. Practical items for different reasons, things a person might need on an adventure through the jungle. The jungle. How many daughters and mothers have canoed the Amazon River together? There we were, living the *Wild Kingdom* adventure. This time there was no television, no thirteen-inch Zenith to fight over. Just us, two butterflies, and a Spanish-English dictionary. "*Dos mariposas es bonitas azul,*" I said.

"*Si.*"

Then finally, the last leg of the journey: a peaceful, twenty-minute paddle in traditional dugout canoes through the swamp to the lodge.

jun•gle: A wilderness of dense overgrowth; a place or situation of ruthless competition. My mother and I have always been competitive with each other, even though we outwardly appear to be opposites. Granola Granny and Girly Girl. But secretly, we vie for some unnamed, intangible prize.

com•pe•ti•tion: My therapist once asked me, "Is your mother jealous of you?"
"I don't know."
"Are you jealous of her?"
"No. We're just so…opposite."

As we approached the lodge, I was shocked to see the locals swimming in the black water, diving from the dock and frolicking without a care. Kids and adults alike played and splashed and laughed, just like the public pool in my hometown. "Aren't there piranhas?" my mother asked our guide. That's when we were told that yes, there are piranhas here, but unless you're gushing blood from a main artery, there's no danger of attack. Evidently there are forty to sixty piranha species, some much more aggressive than others. It's the really aggressive ones we hear about, the ones that make world headlines. The ones featured in Loney Planet. The Tupi devilfish of legend.

Sacha Lodge would be home sweet stilted home for the next several days, the closest thing to luxury one will find in Amazonia. The main building is literally a tree house about six feet above the water—three stories high with a dining room on the bottom floor, a bar on the second floor, a small library on the third floor, and a little observation deck on top. Boardwalks lead to seven duplex-like, thatched-roof cabins. Each room features a flush toilet, hot water (a rarity in this neck of the woods), and screened walls. A generator provides electricity from 6 a.m. until 10 p.m. Accommodations fit for Farrah.

For the first three days in the jungle, I was able to keep up the arduous pace of my diehard travel companions. Before sunrise the first morning, we pulled on our Wellies—knee-high rubber boots—and hiked through the fauna. A bare-chested native guide, a black-haired man with a round face, blazed the way with machete in hand. Bringing up the rear was our other guide, the Australian woman with pointy red hair.

The trail led us through pristine high ground where the rainforest canopy reaches its greatest height. Hundreds of fifty-foot kapok trees towered above, their roots forming huge buttresses and stilts to give support on thin soil. That afternoon, we climbed to the top of a 130-foot observation tower perched above the biggest kapok of all. It was there, high above the canopy, that my mother leaned against the damp wood rail of the observation platform and peered through her binoculars.

"It's a three-toed sloth," she said, giddy with childlike excitement. With an outstretched arm, she pointed in the sloth's general direction while keeping the binoculars pressed firmly against her face. Watching her revel in her discovery reminded me of Marlin Perkins's narration, the episodes we'd watch when I was a kid, how I'd dream of exploring exotic jungles and faraway lands. And now here we were, traipsing among spotted toucans, parrots, monkeys, and snakes.

"This is the life," my mother said when the sloth had finally climbed out of sight, and I agreed.

I realized then that, although we weren't getting along particularly better at that moment than we had during the day, at least we weren't *not* getting along. In fact, we were having a pretty good time. Standing in the sky-high treetop, spotting exotic animals in their natural habitat, we shared an experience, did something that most mothers and daughters would never do. We had embarked on an adventure, and now, in the thick of it, halfway through the journey, the three-toed sloth brought the old *Wild Kingdom* show to life. Real life. Real time. No closed door. No dictionary or heavy sighs. We'd grown past that, at least for now, for this moment.

Twenty-Nine

That evening we all piled into a single dugout canoe to search for caiman, the alligators of South America. In the dead of night we paddled silently through the swamp. With six people in one canoe, it would have been easy to tip over. Our native guide called out in caiman-language grunts—a deep, throaty grumble. And then, when something in the darkness grunted back, a sharp stabbing pain shot from my belly up through my throat. With a flashlight clutched between his teeth and the machete tucked into the waist of his shorts, the guide got out of the boat, walked barefoot through the waist-deep water, and picked up a two-foot-long baby caiman. Its eyes reflected the light and its vertical pupils narrowed to knife-thin slits. The guide clamped the caiman's long, teeth-filled mouth shut with one hand and pinned its writhing tail under his arm. Its glowing yellow eyes made me gasp. "You want to touch?" the guide asked, and brought it over so we could have a look.

I wondered where Momma Caiman was. Any momma of any species will protect its young, will attack and kill any perceived threat. Momma bears will rip a man from limb to limb to protect their cubs. Momma humans can lift cars to save their children. My mother would do anything for me. That's what mommas do—they turn off the television, they get their Ph.D. and buy a house and put food on the table. They buy you dictionaries. They make mistakes and they're hard to get along with and they disapprove of things they don't understand. But I understand, so she must have done something right. I understand that we each have our own definitions of what makes a woman. I need not define our relationship by our differences. I understand that my mother saves packets of saltine crackers while I imagine Wonder Woman somersaulting from a crashing plane. And that's okay, it's all okay. That's what mommas do; they remember the *Wild Kingdom* dream and they stuff snacks into fanny packs in case we're hungry later.

"You touch?" the guide said again. How many teeth does a momma caiman have, I wondered. As the guide stepped closer, I protested and squirmed involuntarily. The canoe tipped side to side and almost flipped us out. "No move!" the guide yelled at me, and henceforth I was banned from nighttime canoe rides.

a•dap•ta•tion: The ability of a species to survive in a particular ecological niche, especially because of alterations of form or behavior brought about through natural selection. It's not like the Amazon trip fixed everything. We still annoyed each other plenty, believe me—we still do. But we've learned to work around each other's quirks. Or just give each other space. Every creature requires a certain amount of unencumbered habitat, a zone of no-enter-dom. I stopped slamming the door in my mother's house years ago. Now we find other ways to keep a wide berth, sometimes wider and sometimes narrower, but a tacit agreement exists. And it mostly works.

Thirty

By day three, I'd gotten the hang of jungle life. There are some simple rules to living in Tarzan's kingdom:

a) Everything is sopping wet all the time—your clothes, your bath towel, your bed sheets. Your shirt will actually mold while you're wearing it. There's nothing you can do about this.

b) The drinking water is brown. It's filtered water from the river. The brown is tannin and harmless (so I'm told), so pretend it's flavorless tea and enjoy.

c) The insects are huge. If you wake during the night to find a beetle the size of a dinner plate clinging to the cabin screen or the wall next to your head, don't scream. It will wake Momma Caiman under your boardwalk, and she's already perturbed.

d) Don't wear makeup, not even mascara. It doesn't fit the safari-vest image, and it just slides off in the humidity anyway. Clear lip gloss is okay.

e) A Swiss Army knife is every woman's best friend. Scrape the muck from under your fingernails; trim your bangs; flick dime-sized ants off your pillow and wrestle your crackers from their mandibles.

By day four, I really needed a day off. Between the day hikes and nighttime scary noises, I was worn out. "Go on without me," I told the Rambo chicks as they tromped into the jungle.

My mother reached into her fanny pack and handed me packages of pulverized Saltines. "Here, I saved these for you," she said.

"Thanks. I'm going to nap in my hammock, then do a little Lonely Planet reading. I might even go for a dip—I've seen the locals do it. It's safe."

But now, in the middle of this black lagoon—what a fool, I said to myself.

I was alone in caiman territory. In deep water. How deep? I pulled my arms through the water, but I got nowhere. I wondered how long it would take a school of piranhas to devour my flesh, clean my skeleton of all muscle, tendons, and cartilage. Would my bones float to the surface or settle into the mud? Or I could simply drown out there. Panic and flail and choke. Sink below the surface in a frenzy—down to the dark depths of the Tupi devilfish, like a Domino's Pizza delivery to the underbelly of the Amazon.

What's a girl like me doing in a place like this, I wondered. A girl…like me?

e•vac•u•a•tion: 1) Expulsion, as of contents. 2) Physiology: discharge, as of waste matter through excretory passages, especially from the bowels. 3) Removal of persons from an endangered area. 4) Get me the hell outta here.

Girl like me, I thought.
Lid still on. Ears above water.
There is no other girl like me.

In my head, Marlin Perkins narrated the scene. The camera panned around, focused on me, and *Wild Kingdom*'s sky sang: "… you can count on when the going's rough…."

I was a Charlie's Angel, holding the bad guys at bay. "Freeze, motherfuckers," I said out loud and took another stroke—or maybe I just thought the words.

Arm out, stroke. Lid on. Stroke.

Stand back, all evil fish, all things creepy and crawly. I swim where I dare!

I roared in unison with the howler monkeys above and glided with ease toward the marshy bank.

Stroke and glide.

Because like my mommy said, I am so much *more*.

PART IV

Starry Nights

Thirty-One

Visalia, California (2013)—

My father telephones from Mexico to ask how things are going. I answer in half-truths.

"How's my house?" he asks.

"Great," I tell him. I don't tell him I've let a friend move in for free.

"How's my stuff?"

"Good," I tell him.

I tell him that the one hundred and one legal-size boxes from Office Depot that he packed during his last visit home have been moved into the shed. (Save for a brief return to Visalia several months after the three-week-visit-with-a-vague-return-date-scheme—just long enough to box his belongings—he's stayed in Mexico. So far, so good.) My father still has hopes that my brother will arrange to have the boxes shipped via an international moving company, but the fact that it would cost ten times more to ship the stuff than it would to replace most of it has my brother stalling. I tell my dad that shipping is expensive. I tell him that because my brother lives half of the time here and half of the time there, he might drive to Mexico with my dad's stuff sometime in the (vague) future.

I don't tell him that other than the one hundred and one boxes in the shed, almost everything is gone. My brother and I got rid of the furniture and knick-knacks and clothes and DVDs and magazines and, yes, even the massive porn collection that took up half the garage cabinets. I don't remind him that when he left two-plus years ago he vowed (promised?) he wasn't coming back, not ever, that Mexico would be permanent, that my brother and I should keep or otherwise dispose of his stuff—all his stuff—other than the Office Depot boxes. I don't tell him that we gave much of it away, some to charity, but most—even the porn—to a pair of men fortuitously cruising the neighborhood in a broken-down pickup and asking for scrap metal. It was their lucky day. I don't tell him we did this to make room for my friend. I don't tell him we let my friend move in as barter for maintaining the place, how David and I are planning things out for when David moves to Mexico for good, how I'm up to my eyeballs as it is and maintaining yet another a vacant house will put me over the edge. I don't tell him about my friend moving in because I don't want to hurt his feelings. I don't tell him for fear he'll get territorial and rush back to Visalia, to his rightful house, to his boxes, to me.

"How's your mom?" he asks.

I tell him I'm in the middle of cleaning out Mom's house in Three Rivers because she'll never live there again, and it's a huge mess because she's a lifelong hoarder, you know, and the junk's piled sky high inside and out like in the old sitcom *Sanford and Son*—not to mention the rats' nests in the enclosed porch where Mom used to sleep on cool summer nights, oh my God I think she slept among rats, and the rodent poop, how it's all over her art studio, in every junk-filled box and on every pile of old papers and in between papers and inside boxes of dried paints, and junk and junk and junk, and old photos, and junk, and wadded clothes jammed between this and that, and junk and dust, and why are there random dishes and silverware in the box with extension cords and income tax returns and unopened boxes of Kleenex and canned corn, and did I mention the rat poop and junk, or maybe it's mice, you know hantavirus is a life-threatening disease spread to humans through contact with contaminated dust from mice droppings and it's really dusty out there in the art studio and I've had a headache for days—and it's a forty-minute drive each direction from her house to mine and I don't have time for the house-cleaning project or my school or my job, what with taking her to therapy and the doctors and keeping her engaged each day so she does more than watch the paint peel from the walls—and to make it a thousand times worse, she's a complete and utter pill when I try to engage her because she doesn't want to be engaged, she just wants to be left alone in the dark and not be spoken to, but she does want me to hover over her and fill her cup with peach Snapple and adjust her pillow and wiggle her big toe and smooth her blanket—just not talk to her while I do it—in other words, even though she's officially out of my house, even with the paid caregivers on duty—thank God we can afford the as-sisted living—I'm still a caregiver/slave and I might be stretched a little thin right now, and well, to be honest, I don't sleep well at night—in fact I hardly sleep at all and I haven't for a year now since she had the aortic dissection and succession of strokes and the ICUs and hospitals and rehab hospitals and skilled nursing facilities and then home health care at my house, and then finally, thank God for assisted living and everyone who's helped—the nurses, the therapists, my husband, Aunt Tonya, Mom's best friend, the other few friends I haven't managed to alienate because I've pretty much dropped out of sight what with all these new respon-sibilities that have taken over my life, and how I get annoyed even with people trying to help, even my friends or Mom's friends who are older and wiser and full of advice because, you know, I get tired of everyone giving me advice when they haven't lived a single day in my life…they tell me what I need to do, *you need to blah-blah-blah* they say, but they don't really fucking know what it takes, I mean *really* takes, and how most of it doesn't work and there are only so many hours in the goddamn day—well, they all tell me I'm a bit edgy (no fucking kidding) and that perhaps, just perhaps, I should go back to yoga or take a day off or get an anti-anxiety prescription. Like maybe Xanax.

"Oh, Carole, I'm so sorry," he says. "I wish there was something I could do to help your mom." And then he starts to cry. He says he wants to be by her side, just lie down on the floor next to her bed and tell her how much he loves her. "Do you think she would understand?" he asks. "Maybe that would help her get better. Should I fly back to see her?"

I tell my father now's not a good time to visit.

When I study that old photo, the one I showed my mother recently, the one of four-year-old me standing next to the laundry basket wearing my mother's bra, I imagine what fills the penumbra, the unseen area that lies beyond the framed border. I imagine my father, young again, holding the camera to his eye, his finger pushing the lever, the square flashcube illuminating the room while the aperture clicks open, then shut. I imagine the contents of my parents' house back then, the silverware with little starbursts patterned into the handles and the reel-to-reel tape recorder and the peace-sign pendent in my father's bottom desk drawer—and how, like all of us, my parents accumulated and periodically purged throughout their lives, purged during their moves from house to house, their shifts from marriage to divorce, from phases of interest to disinterest, from hobby to hobby, from career goals to accomplishments and compromised settlements. I imagine the one hundred and one boxes currently in my father's shed and wonder how he decided what was worthy of packing, worthy of saving. When I think about the decision process my father must have gone through—what to keep and what to discard, and the fact that he did so with the knowledge that he's coming close to the end of his life—well, this prompts me to reflect on my own life, decisions I've made, things I've acquired or let go, whether or not I've acquired the right contents for my life, tangible or otherwise.

Knowledge of our eventual death requires that we pay attention to life. The situation we find ourselves in—not just the fact that we die, but how incredibly rich the world is, how many things it offers us—demands that we manage the many choices we have in our relatively short lifespan. We've got this burden of figuring out what things are most worth going after, knowing, consciously or not, that someday we'll look back and possibly discover we didn't make the best choices. Although we have the chance for some do-overs, both in terms of our goals and our strategies for reaching them, we've got to be careful.

Okay, I'm paying attention. I'm trying to be careful. Swimming alone in the Amazon River might not be strategically sound, but to me, the experience—the challenge—was an important activity to engage in. Following my father through the Mexican desert of Cataviña, poking the sand for rattlesnakes—okay, the odds are a little dicey again. Worth the risk? The answer depends on what I'm trying to do with my life.

What adds value to our lives is the content of our lives—what should we fill our lives with? Sure, we want to pack in as much stuff as we can. But what's really worth going after? The way I see it, there are two different strategies.

- **Strategy #1:** Given the dangers of failure if you aim too ambitiously, you should settle for the kinds of goals that you're virtually guaranteed you'll accomplish. The pleasures of food, company, sex, hot fudge sundaes: eat, drink, and be merry. Pack in lots of small pleasures.

- **Strategy #2:** The first option is all well and good—you've got a pretty high chance of succeeding. The trouble is, those are small potatoes. Some of the most valuable things life don't come so readily, and there are no guarantees you'll achieve them. You might want to write a novel, compose a symphony, solve the biological mysteries of macro-evolution and punctuated equilibrium theory, or, for that matter, raise a family. Some fans of strategy number two might argue that these things are the most valuable things life can offer, that a life filled with these is more valuable than a life filled with small potatoes.

But if you had a guarantee—if God or the Universe or the Random Force Behind Sitting-up Mud said, "I promise you'll get the life you want. Would you rather have your blip-of-a-life filled with food and drink, or do you want a life filled with accomplishment?"—you might say the life filled with accomplishment holds more value. The trouble is, of course, a life aiming for greater accomplishments is also a life with a greater chance of failure. You aim to write the great American novel, and ten years later you decide you don't have it in you. Your article detailing the evolution of the arachnid internal skeleton of scorpions doesn't make quite the academic splash you'd hoped for. You have no children, and now that you're caring for your elderly parents—often begrudgingly—you wonder who will do the same for you someday, and wouldn't that be the end-all-be-all of just deserts for your ungrateful, unenthusiastic attitude? *Spectrum of reconciliation*, my ass. Buck up, sister. Find a damn place to stand and occupy the space with intent—are you in the cave, or out? I wonder who will clean out the contents of my empty house.

So what's the right strategy to take? I suppose many of us would say there's another option:

- **Strategy #3:** Get the right mixture. Aim for a certain number of large potatoes. Go for some large accomplishments, because if you manage to pull them off, your life will have more value. But also throw in a smattering of small potatoes—at least then, big-potato harvest or not, you're assured of something.

Most of us would agree to the benefits of Strategy #3. But what is the right mixture?

Thirty-Two

San Vicente, Mexico (1994)—

It wasn't the first time I'd heard his Big Bang monologue on the origins of the universe, nor would it be the last, but it was the first time I really listened to his words, and the first time I noticed the Big Bang sequence playing out before my eyes—in a town, a person, a life. In San Vicente, I caught my first glimpse of what I'd come to recognize as the "somethingness-that-erupts-from-nothingness" in one man's world, and the subsequent detonations that fire again and again, yet with slightly greater velocity each time.

My father and I had just begun our *Tuesdays with Morrie* play-it-by-ear road trip through Baja, and night number one was upon us. We drove along Mexican Federal Highway 1 in the dark. From where I sat behind the wheel, the black sky had fused with the horizon so tightly that the distinction between earth and sky ceased to exist. Bone-dry air pounded through the open windows of the car, drowning out the music tinning from the tape deck. From the dashboard speakers, Don McLean crooned his vigil to Vincent Van Gogh in the song "Starry, Starry Night" (we practically wore out the *American Pie* cassette during that trip, so if "Starry, Starry Night" wasn't actually playing at that moment, it was at least stuck in my head). We should have stopped for the night an hour ago, back in Ensenada or perhaps Rosarito Beach. Never drive at night—rule number one in Mexico, where dark roads are notorious for potholes, meandering animals, and gun-toting bandits. The perpetual desolation of the Baja Desert seemed to go on forever, and for a long time the headlights' dim glow did nothing more than illuminate the emptiness ahead.

When we rolled into the dusty town of San Vicente, its explosion of activity and light sprang from the barren land like an oasis. It wasn't the sort of town that attracted tourists. I imagine most Americans would visit only by default while driving the trans-peninsular highway on their way to someplace else. We inched along the two-lane highway, which was the one and only paved street in the town, past stray dogs and food carts and pickup beds loaded with passengers, kids playing soccer in the dirt, and men sprawled in white plastic chairs that leaned against turquoise stucco walls. Maybe a couple hundred souls populated this town, with its one Pemex gas station, one grocery store, a couple of tire shops, an auto mechanic, two sit-down restaurants, and lighted pole signs blaring *Tecate*, *Coca-Cola*, and *Pharmacia*. Despite its bleak appearance, the town teemed with life. The air was full of pedestrian chatter and exhaust and music and the smell of roasting corn.

My father did all the talking at the motel counter. I don't speak Spanish fluently, but I recognized enough words to get the gist of the conversation. Just as the town seemed to burst from the nothingness of the nighttime desert, my father sprang forth in his interactions with the motel clerk.

Yes, the woman said, *we have a room available, and no, the beds do not have fleas.*

I didn't know if was customary to ask about fleas, but the question struck me as a bit odd. We weren't yet twenty-four hours into this getting-to-know-you excursion, so I wasn't quite sure what to expect, either from my father or from the circumstances.

My father asked the young woman her name, then proceeded to fill her in on our situation…and then some. *This is my thirty-year-old daughter, Carolina,* he said in Spanish, pronouncing my "Spanish" name "Cat-o-leen-a." *She lives in Central California where she teaches elementary school. My wife, Marina, is Mexican, but she's at home in Southern California with my other daughter, Liza. I have two daughters and one son, but only one daughter from my Mexican wife. Carolina here, she doesn't speak Spanish. She tells me she took French in high school, but of course, that doesn't do her any good here in Mexico, does it? Ha, ha!*

Okay, Dad, time to wrap up, I thought.

The young woman and my father went back and forth for several minutes, but the conversation moved too quickly for me to pick out anything more than a few of the major words. It seemed like he was giving our life stories to this stranger. *I'm a professor,* he said of himself. *I have been speaking Spanish for forty years. My wife doesn't enjoy traveling like I do. The car is packed with camping gear but we decided to get a room for the night. Do you think our gear will be safe from thieves in the parking lot, or should we empty the car's contents and take everything to the room?*

Jesus H. Christ, is that a wise thing to ask, I wondered.

Before my father asked how much the room would cost, he opened his wallet, which bulged so wide with its dozens of credit cards that he kept a rubber band around it. He removed the rubber band, flopped the wallet open, and fanned out the paper bills so the corner of each bill and its numerical imprint extended from the billfold slit to reveal one thousand dollars in American twenty-dollar bills.

Do you take American cash?

Yes, of course.

Splendid. How much for the night?

Thirty-Three

After settling into the room, we unfolded our camping chairs out in the courtyard and uncorked a bottle of red wine, eager to watch what the news had promised would be a minor but vivid meteor shower. As we watched the night sky, my father continued the cosmology lecture he'd started earlier in the day, one he'd touch on not only during our trip but for the next two decades, a conversation he resumes every chance he gets, even to this day.

"Billions of stars," he said with his face turned up to the sky, his neck resting along the back of his chair. "We live in the Milky Way galaxy." He pronounced it *mill*-kk-ee way, with such emphasis on the "l" and hard "k" that it sounded like a totally different word than "milky."

"Yes, I know."

"There are so many things you don't know. Can I tell you?"

As he spoke, I noticed the young woman from behind the check-in counter was now standing under the patio cover across from us in the courtyard, washing laundry by hand in a big tub. Out near the road, several men had gathered to socialize, some leaning back in their white plastic chairs, others propped against the open back of a flatbed truck. Although I could not make out the words, their conversation lilted in a jovial tone. Friday night, time to unwind. *Uno mas cerveza.*

"All the stars you see are part of the Milky Way galaxy. Its name derives from the hazy band of white light in the sky, the milky clouds arching over us. The Milky Way is shaped like a disc," he said, and motioned with his hands, "bulging at its bar-shaped core, with arms spiraling outward. It's one hundred thousand light-years in diameter, one thousand light-years thick, and contains four hundred billion stars."

I filled our thermos camping mugs with wine.

"Our planet sits close to the inner rim of one of those arms," he said, "which means we're near the outer edge of the galaxy itself. And even though we can't feel it, our galaxy rotates at four hundred miles per second."

I imagined what it might be like to be the galaxy itself, if the galaxy were a conscious being—spinning around and around, a whirling dervish with arms extended, fanned outward into the abyss.

"Which means you're hurling through space at the same rate," he said.

I sat up in my chair and spread a blanket on the ground. What better way to take in the narration than to gaze straight up into the heavens, like a narrated slide show? "I'm gonna lay down," I said.

"No," he said, referring to my grammar. "Lay and lie. Lay requires a direct object. So you lie down on the ground. One says, 'I lie down, but I lay the book down.'"

"Whatever."

"Say it: 'I will lie down.'"

"It doesn't matter."

"Yes, it matters," he insisted.

We'd had this conversation twice today already. "It only matters in written speech. Nobody cares when you're talking out loud."

"I care. You should care. My fifth-grade teacher, Ms. Loretta Swift, she cared. And she had perfect grammar."

"She died a spinster." Which was true. We'd talked about Ms. Swift that day, too. "Now she's cold, dead, and alone." I sat back up and gulped my mug of wine.

The woman doing laundry hunched over the tub, her shoulders rising and falling, her arms extended, submerged in water. The men out front whooped at what must have been the punch line to a story, their laughter punctuated with the pop-fizz, pop-fizz of *Tecate*.

"Say, 'I lie down,'" he said.

I pointed to the sky. "There. A shooting star. Did you see it?"

"Yes. That's a meteor, though, not really a star. It's a fragment the size of a grain of sand burning up in the atmosphere. The stars are constant."

"I know. More wine?"

He repeated almost word for word what he'd said in the car. "Before the Big Bang, there were no stars. The universe was created by a cosmic Big Bang 13.7 billion years ago. Before that, there was an infinity of nothingness. That's one of great mysteries: how we got from nothingness to somethingness. Starting with the chaos of radiation at over one hundred billion degrees Kelvin, in a universe initially smaller than a single atom, the universe started to expand. It blasted outward, and then cooled as it expanded. There was no actual bang because there were no ears to hear a bang."

"How do you know there was no sound if you weren't there to hear it?" I wiseacred. But it fell on deaf ears.

"After a tenth of a second—are you listening?—just one tenth of one second—subatomic particles condensed from pure energy: electrons, positrons, neutrinos and antineutrinos, photons—by which time the temperature had cooled to thirty billion degrees Kelvin. By the time the universe was two seconds old, neutrons formed, and a neutron can decay into a proton and an electron, although not all of them did. By the time the universe cooled to four billion degrees, the first hydrogen atoms appeared, followed by heavy hydrogen and tritium; then, fusion of these particles produced helium atoms."

I tried to imagine how lonely it must have been before the bang—how absolute nothingness, how complete solitude, how utter darkness and total seclusion would feel. And then all of a sudden: pop! The joy of activity—little nano-things buzzing about. But if I were the universe, and if I had been used to solitude—if all I had known was solitude—would I like the nano-things buzzing about, or would I find their chatter mundane and annoying?

"The first stars were huge, much larger than our sun, and they were composed almost entirely of hydrogen. No new hydrogen is formed in the stars. They fuse hydrogen in their cores to produce helium. When the hydrogen runs out, the tremendous temperature allows helium atoms to fuse up to iron. Atoms heavier than iron are not produced until the star explodes, at which time the heavy atoms are blown out into space, where they are incorporated into new stars. Our Sun is calculated to be a third-generation star because it has all the heavy atoms, up to uranium. Atoms heavier than uranium are so radioactive that they decay into lighter elements. The atomic number of uranium is 92. Atomic physicists have produced man-made transuranium atoms up to number 118. I have memorized the names of all 118 elements in the order of their atomic numbers. Reciting them each day is a kind of meditative exercise that gives me access to the throne of the Creator."

"Huh." It was all I could think to respond.

The woman rinsed her laundry using a hose and a second wash basin, then began passing it through rubber rollers to squeeze out the water with a contraption that reminded me of the old wringer washer my great-grandmother had used.

"You came from this nothingness, Carole. You originated in the Big Bang. Your very existence was improbable, in that each cosmic bifurcation that could have led to a no-Carole universe providentially favored you. There were millions of events that could have otherwise led to a no-Carole universe. For example, if gravity had been just 0.02 percent stronger, the stars would have burned themselves out before human life could evolve. Likewise, if gravity had been just 0.02 percent weaker, there would be no galaxies or stellar systems, no oceans and no people. It turns out that the entire cosmos is tailor-made to accommodate human evolution. This is a stunning insight called the anthropic principle. The observations of the physical universe must be compatible with the conscious life that observes it."

"Um, okay."

"I want you to understand this," he said, referring to cosmic principles. He paused for a moment as he looked at the sky. "I'm sorry I couldn't send you to Stanford," he finally said.

My father got his master's and doctorate at Stanford, yet never contributed a single penny toward my education. I worked full time (and my mother ran her credit cards sky high) to get through the local community college and state university. The possibility of a private school like Stanford never even entered my universe.

"A particular school is irrelevant. Anyway, I wouldn't have wanted to go, not at that time in my life. So, the chances of events?"

He continued with his previous train of thought. "If the Earth had no continents, there would be no you. If there had been no moon, there would be no you. If the Earth had not been struck by an asteroid sixty-five million years ago, there would be no humans or other primates. My point is that if any of the laws of nature or timing of cosmic historical events had been different, there would be no humans and no Carole."

A pair of stray dogs meandered into the men's circle. One of the guys bent to pet them, and someone turned up the music, which seemed to come from a radio inside the hotel lobby, or perhaps a boom box just outside the arched corridor. The woman hung her laundry on a line inside the courtyard. She called something to one the men out front, and one of the men called something back.

"I'm so glad I can talk to you about these things, Carole, because my wife is not interested at all." He often referred to Marina as "my wife," even to me, though I'd known her some fourteen or fifteen years.

"Yes, that's what you always say." I'd heard it a million times. "What's Marina interested in?"

"She likes to cook and clean. She's a wonderful cook, you know. Makes everything from scratch. And she keeps the house spotless, for which I am grateful. She treats me like a king. But she doesn't have an intellectual bone in her body."

"What does she do when she's not cooking and cleaning?" Marina kept the house immaculate, all right, everything scrubbed and polished to a shine. She waited on my father hand and foot like a servant, hunched over the stove, her face moist with perspiration, stirring and serving from the heavy iron pots, stepping back and forth from the stove to the table and back to the stove again, while my father inhaled his food. She did it all, like a maid-cook-servant, never sitting to eat until my father had had his fill, until he'd licked his plate with his tongue and followed it up with one last shot of tequila. *More tortillas?* she'd ask him in Spanish. Even after three decades of living in the States with my father, she would never learn to speak English with ease, for she and my father spoke only Spanish at home.

"Well, she goes to the grocery store. Does laundry. That sort of thing."

"What about for fun?"

"For her, that's fun."

"That's not fun," I said.

"She lives and breathes to serve my every need. That's what makes her happy, for which I am eternally grateful. I suppose I couldn't ask for a better wife." He took in a deep breath. "Except that I wish she was interested in cosmology. And evolution and philosophy."

We watched another shooting star.

"The Sun is a star at the center of the solar system," he says. "It's more than a hundred times bigger than Earth, and it's made up mostly of hydrogen and helium." He counted out each item on his fingers to make sure he got them all. "Hydrogen, helium, and trace amounts of oxygen, carbon, iron, neon, nitrogen, silicon, magnesium, and sulfur."

Thirty-Four

When I reflect on that night now, I'm struck by my father's in-tellectual ability to reverse-engineer the cosmos, making me the focus of a Carole-centric universe—a rendition that, to be hon-est, I find both comforting and annoying. The Big Bang theory is, after all, the latest in a litany of creation myths, humankind's ongoing attempt to describe the ordering of the cosmos—we have, for example, creation-from-chaos stories like the Sumerians' Eridu Genesis, and the Greeks' Theogony of Hesiod; the Earth-driver type like the Cherokee story of the water beetle who formed the Earth from mud; emergence myths like the Mayan account of two gods, Kukulkan and Tepeu, who, after failing to create humans from mud, then wood, finally constructed man from maize; out-of-nothing explanations like the Judeo-Christian story of Genesis, or the collection of myths emanating from Ancient Egypt; world-parent tales like Rangi and Papa from the South Pacific, or the Hindu account of Mahapralaya and Svayambhu. Like my father, I could go on (and on and on), but my point is that we humans want to know where we came from. We want to know the ori-gins of the universe. And for some of us, we want to know more about our family of origin. Where did I come from in the big and small scheme of things—I, the mysteriously generated organism that emanated from a long-ago crashing of atoms, but also I, the daughter of Bruce and Aranga Firstman.

My father's version of the origin of the universe intrigues me, not only because it includes me, by name even, and not only because it locates the temporarily clustered atoms that form the me I recognize in the mirror—the physical body I temporarily inhabit during this blip I call a lifetime—but also because this version accounts for the longevity of my atoms, the basic elements that spewed into existence billions of years before now, elements that will still exist long after my body's gone: a form of immortality, I suppose—not quite as comforting as the notion of heavenly eternal life, but at least the element-recycling plot of the Big Bang storyline is, well, it's something. Better than nothing.

I admire the fact that my father, through his professional pursuits—researching the anatomical features of modern scorpions in order to support Darwin's theory of evolution, thus contributing to the ongoing discourse of the creationist-evolutionist debate—adds to humankind's inquiry of nature, science, and God. That's big-potatoes stuff, the Strategy #2 approach in the Contents for Life conundrum.

I find comfort in the fact that my father and I share the same DNA.

If he can tackle big potatoes, then maybe I can, too.

I'm annoyed by the fact that my father and I share the same DNA.

If he can tackle big potatoes, then why didn't Raising a Family make his big-potatoes list?

Technically speaking, my father spent significantly more time with my half-sister, Liza, than he did with my brother and me. But the difference was in physical proximity rather than genuine day-to-day interest. Although my dad and Liza lived under the same roof for twenty years (until she died of cancer two days before her twentieth birthday), I don't think he was much more involved in her upbringing than he was in my brother's and mine. Children are seen and not heard. Children are the mother's responsibility. Don't bother me while I'm in my office at the far end of the house. Close the door on your way out.

Fathering a child and raising a child are two very different things. Mating with a woman and being a husband are two very different things. (Recall our humanoid friend Chaka from *Land of the Lost*, how he *went home, banged Mrs. Chaka, and probably his newly widowed sister-in-law, Mrs. Tuktuk, as well.* Chaka mated. Judging from the behavior of most primates I've observed, I doubt he did much fathering.) On an intellectual level, I know it's the Asperger's that drives my father's paternal disinterest. He's hardwired this way. He can't help it. On the other hand, relatively newfound medical labels are a weak salve for old emotional wounds.

As my dad and I sat in the courtyard of that Mexican motel watching the meteor shower, as he spoke—or perhaps I should say, lectured—about crashing atoms and radioactive decay and anthropic principle, while we sipped red wine from thermos camping mugs, his apparent disinterest in the domestic activities going on around us mirrored his lifelong disregard for my own family of origin, my mother, my brother and me (and Marina and Liza, too); I never ranked as a big potato. On a personal, day-to-day level, he is and always has been the center of his own universe. So I'm unsatisfied with my father's particular potato salad recipe.

My own mixture of small and large potatoes might not be any better, though. Here I am, midlife: no kids; no symphonies; no correspondence addressed to me from Stephen J. Gould; strained relationships with my elderly parents; still searching for my spot on the spectrum of reconciliation as I pack and shuffle their Office Depot boxes from house to shed, from house to assisted-living apartment. Good daughter or bad? *Who will clean out the contents of my house?*

Thirty-Five

(2013)—

My mother asks to see some of the old photographs in the box I've brought to her assisted-living apartment, so I give her a stack of four-by-six-inch glossies, a small portion from the Ecuador adventure she and I shared.

"Here," I say. "Galapagos and Amazon."

She holds them in her right hand, the only functional one now, which is doubly awkward because she'd been left-handed before the stroke. Keeping the stack in one hand, she shuffles through with her thumb and index finger for about twenty seconds, then fixes her gaze on the blanket wrapped around her feet. She's already lost interest. The cognitive damage manifests itself, among other ways, in a short attention span. And deep depression.

To keep her engaged, I ask if the photos are in chronological order. She fingers the stack and determines that no, they are not in order, and when I suggest she get them in order she snaps at me. "Carole, I can't."

"You can."

"No, I can't," she says, her barbed words sharp with disdain.

It would be easier for me to put the photos in order myself, or to simply drop them back into the box as is. But I want my mother to redevelop her cognitive skills—not to mention her fine and gross motor skills—so that she might learn to do things for herself again. If only she could regain some independence, I tell myself, it would improve her quality of life on a grand scale. So I'm prompting her to help herself. She need not waste away in the recliner, pushing the call button around her neck each time she wants the blanket rearranged, the thermostat adjusted, or to go to the toilet. If she wanted to, she could get better. I want her to get better. Although she's come so far in the last year, since the emergency room when I told her goodbye forever, this is not the ending I would have chosen for her life.

Remember those *Choose Your Own Adventure* books from the 1980s and '90s? My third-grade students ate 'em up. I still have a few of those books stored in boxes in my attic—stuff I saved in case I decided to go back to teaching elementary school someday.

It's a series of interactive chapter books written from a second-person point of view where the reader assumes the role of protagonist in each adventure—the private investigator, the spy, the archeologist—and makes choices that determine the plot's outcome. Typically, a substantial story setup comes to some sort of a pivot, a fork in the road. Every few pages, the protagonist faces two or three options, each of which leads to more options. You have to make a choice. Which will ultimately lead to more choices.

If I remember correctly, it was my little friend Tyler (cannibalizing-scorpions illustrator extraordinaire: *"Any questions?"*) who suggested *The Cave of Time* for read-aloud period, when I'd read aloud for thirty minutes after lunch each day. The story details are fuzzy now, but I seem to recall the main character hiking in Snake

Canyon for the first few pages, when…you find yourself lost in the strange, dimly lit Cave of Time. Inside, you find two passageways. One curves downward to the right, the other leads upward to the left. You realize that the one leading down may take you into the past, and the one leading up may go to the future. Which will you choose? If you take the left passage, turn to page twenty. If you take the right branch, turn to page sixty-one. If you take the third option, which is to turn around and step back outside the cave, go to page twenty-one. Whichever you choose, be careful. In the Cave of Time, you might end up face to face with a hungry Tyrannosaurus Rex, or be lured aboard an alien spaceship.

This choice-leads-to-choice structure is consistent, but the choices are tricky because most of the time neither choice seems terribly more promising than the other—take the canoe or hike the hill? And yet, inevitably, one of those choices leads to an early ending: death for the really exciting books—or getting rescued by a police officer for the tamest. But either way, an ending.

At my suggestion, my mother spreads the photos over the blanket on her lap. She groups them by category in little stacks: hoards of iguanas sprawled across volcanic rocks at the ocean's edge; frigatebirds in flight, their outstretched wings black and angular and almost geometric the way they come to a knife-like point at each tip, circling above the sailing mast like prehistoric pterodactyls in search of prey; anacondas wrapped around tree branches, poised high above the nose of the dugout canoe in the photo's foreground.

The canoe. Our chosen mode of transportation in the Amazon. By day we paddled through brown muddy water in search of flora, fauna, and adventure. And later, in the dead of night, we ventured out for caiman. *With a flashlight clutched between his teeth and the machete tucked in the waist of his shorts, the guide got out of the boat, walked barefoot through the waist-deep water, and picked up a two-foot-long baby caiman. Its eyes reflected the light and its vertical pupils narrowed to knife-thin slits. "You touch?" the guide asked.*

In my book, a baby caiman, even with its hideous mouth clenched tight by the guide, ranks right up there with snakes. No can do.

But I did. I touched a baby caiman with my index finger, for the briefest moment.

Why? To orchestrate my own adventure, I suppose. To say I did it and lived to tell about it.

Still, I worried. I squirmed, involuntarily, tipping the boat side to side. *How many teeth does a momma caiman have? And where is she now? Any momma of any species will protect its young, will attack and kill any perceived threat.*

And what about the baby's protective instincts? Might the baby lash out, wriggle free of the guide's bare arms in an attempt to protect its mother? Does that protective instinct work both ways? Is it reciprocal? If the baby perceives me as a threat, it could lunge for my outstretched finger, my arm, my body leaning over the water toward it. Who's to say that baby caiman wouldn't do anything to protect its mother?

Right before my finger pressed against the baby's body, right before the click of physical contact, I had regrets. What if I had just made the wrong decision? What if touching the caiman was the last thing I'd ever do?

My students loved being able to choose those endings (during read-aloud we'd take a class vote, or students like Tyler, who devoured the stories, flipped furiously from one page to the next each morning during silent reading time), but what I loved more was being able to go back and choose the path we didn't choose the first time. The ability to retrace our steps and try again. The canoe in the story seemed so appealing and adventurous at the time, but we had no idea it would lead to an early demise. How could we have known? (Well, I had a pretty strong hunch, actually. But I'm not the publisher's target demographic.)

I doubt that nine-year-old Tyler was able to spot the controlling formula that ran throughout the series. Based on the page number, the concept of the road less traveled, and knowing that most kids reading the book would choose the canoe, the real story is about curiosity and risk. It's safer to stay on the riverbank, to hike the hill—but a canoe sounds much more adventurous.

I don't remember my students or myself regretting choosing the canoe, only to end up dead. It's easy when you've got a book in your hands, when you can flip back and forth with words that never really affect you. You can die a thousand times, put the book down and pick up another.

If only life were like that.

I must live with my decisions. Each time my father calls from Mexico to say that he wants to move back to Visalia, or at least return for an extended visit, I punt—tell him why now's not a good time, how he can't afford it, how his money is tight, I'm too busy taking care of my mother, that maybe later would be better. He sighs into the phone and says he won't be any trouble, and he promises to look after himself when he gets here. That scorpion, the one in a jar—it's still on the table next to my desk. The liquid is even lower than it was when I took it from his office a while back. I keep meaning to add more alcohol, but I've never made the effort. If I'd just make the time, the scorpion would remain pickled, mummified indefinitely. But to be honest, the thought of unscrewing the lid stops me dead—what if it smells? Or what if opening the jar lets in fresh oxygen, enough to hasten the process of decomposition? Or what if none of that bad stuff happens—the scorpion does not stink, the oxygen does not turn the scorpion to dust—what if the truth is that I just don't want to be bothered? What if I'm just too damn lazy to put forth the effort? What if it's all about me—a Carole-centric excuse that supports my Carole-centric life? Instead of staring at the scorpion through the jar, instead of writing a whole goddam book about it, should I pay more attention to the creature itself? I've intellectualized this scorpion for over a hundred pages now, but I've never taken the time, the effort to replenish its jar with the only substance that will keep it intact.

Good daughter or bad?

My canoe has crashed, and it seems that the story really ends here. I can't go back and take the bank of the river. I chose the canoe.

As my mother sorts photographs on her lap, I choose to withhold a bit of information. A few hours ago, I learned that one of her colleagues passed away—Dr. H, a math and science professor with whom she shared an office for many years, died in his sleep. On Facebook, my friend Steve posted:

Jan 5, 2013: My dad passed away in his sleep this morning. He'd been suffering from end-stage diabetes for years, and he spent the last year and a half in a rest home as his body decayed. I told him a few times—never enough in the end—that I appreciated him as a model teacher. From him I learned that striving to be an excellent educator is a noble pursuit. Because of him I teach and I love doing so. I wish I'd had more time with him to tell him these things again and again, but his suffering is over now, and for that I am even more grateful. Currently, we have no plans for a memorial service because he was a private person and asked not to have one, but if plans change, I will update here and in person. Thank you in advance for your prayers and thoughts. I'm going off the radar for a while.

Off the radar.

Yes, I understand. Since my mother's stroke a year ago and her ensuing series of life-or-death crises that have overwhelmed my life, I've been off the radar myself. With the exception of a select few, I've dropped out of practically everything and everyone: I quit my job as teaching associate at the university, dropped most of my graduate school classes (I was both a grad student and a flunky TA at the time of this writing—in the middle of one of those midlife do-overs, transforming myself from third-grade teacher to English professor), shunned my friends, ignored most emails, phone calls, and Facebook messages. Not by choice, but out of necessity. I was needed at the hospitals, the doctors' offices, the therapy gyms, the estate planner's office, the bank, the attorney's desk, the nursing home dining rooms, my spare bedroom turned mother's new quarters, the hallway outside the intensive care nurses' station at five o'clock each morning where the doctors meet for their rounds. An instinctual drive overtook my entire body—I could not have stayed away if I'd tried. I suppose my going off the radar was a choice, but it seemed more like instinct.

But why not tell my mother about Dr. H's death? Why withhold this information? For the same reason I never uttered the word "goodbye" in the emergency room while the nurses prepped her for surgery. Because I want her to get better. It's that weird way I used to think of Farrah Fawcett, how I refused to watch the TV special following her death: if you don't think about cancer, you don't have as much chance of getting it. Logically, it makes no sense. Even icons die.

In my formative years, Farrah was it—the big Wow—an infallible superstar. I suppose my mom is my superstar, strained as our relationship has been. And my dad, too. I mean, something must have clicked. Both my parents were teachers. I am a teacher. Becoming a teacher, for me, didn't seem like a choice—rather, it seemed like the only logical path to take, the only career noble enough, worthy of my pursuit. Teaching is a big potato.

When she tires of sorting photos (which sustains her attention for about ten minutes), I put in a DVD of *Monk*, the cozy whodunit detective series that she used to enjoy before the stroke. Forgetting I'm still in the room with her (her brain ignores everything to her left), she clicks the episode off halfway through. When I ask, "Oh, are we done?" she looks startled.

"I didn't know you were still here."

"I'm here, but I can leave if you want."

"I'd like to get in bed and take a nap."

"Don't you want to see how the story ends?"

"Not really." She pauses. Then she clicks the television back on and apologizes. "That wasn't very nice of me."

Thinking of others. Her brain is starting to work. I cling to moments like this.

"No problem," I say. "I'll stay till the end of the show, then I'll leave so you can be alone."

"Good."

I'm not sure if "good" refers to my staying a while or my leaving soon. Probably the latter. If I help her into bed, I'll verbally coach her through the process so she can spread the blanket and cover her feet herself—the blanket-spreading will take four or five minutes. If she gets into bed after I leave, the caregivers will do it all for her—blanket-spreading done in three seconds.

As the episode nears its conclusion, I fire up my laptop and check my Facebook newsfeed. My friend has twenty-nine responses. I add mine: "Oh, Steve, I am so sorry. Thinking of you."

Thirty-Six

I question my mother's quality of life in the rest home. And I question the decisions I've made over the past year, and whether those decisions have bettered or worsened her existence. Every emergency room event, every surgery, hospitalization, nursing-home admittance—in each situation, the nurses and/or doctors ask the same question, either verbally, in hushed tones while we huddle in the hallway, or in writing, as part of the admittance paperwork: If the patient's heart or breathing were to stop, should the patient be resuscitated or allowed a natural death?

I also wonder about the less dramatic situations, the day-to-day moments over the past year. For months I (and other family members) have coaxed her, almost forced her to eat, to lift her head, open her eyes and see the hallway walls as I wheeled her through the hospital corridors in what they call the "pink chair" (which is really an elevated bed on wheels). She didn't want to do any of this. Her damaged brain wanted to retreat, to sleep, simply withdraw from the world. If left to wither away in her bed, she would have spiraled into a vegetative state, then death. A year later, she's far from vegetative; she's alert and cognizant, and with assistance she can even walk a little. But I question her quality of life, and my responsibility for her present situation.

And then there's my father. I suppose he really is better off in Mexico. His lifestyle—the taxis, the pedestrian-friendly street life, relatives in his town—allows for so much more independence than if he returned to my quiet suburban neighborhood. Then why can't I sleep following a phone call from him?

I wonder if we can quantify the quality of life.

If you had to choose between a long and uneventful life and a short but exciting life, which would you pick? And how would you arrive at that decision? Can you reduce such questions to purely objective, formulaic equations?

Allow me to explore this notion. And just for kicks, let's take it to the absurd.

Surely, I owe my propensity for teaching to my parents. It's in my blood. So what follows are my hypothetical lecture handouts on "Quantifying the Quality of Life." Pretend we're in my college classroom and pretend it's a philosophy class on death. Or life. Keep in mind that I don't actually teach such a class—I'm not a philosopher. Just humor me.

Okay—so you've been handed a packet, the pages of which comprise the remainder of this chapter.

HANDOUT PACKET FOR TODAY'S LECTURE:
"CAN WE QUANTIFY THE QUALITY OF LIFE?"

Here's what we'll discuss on the following pages:

Please note—
Mathematical formulas will NOT be on the test. So relax.

1. TODAY'S DISCUSSION QUESTION:
CAN WE QUANTIFY THE QUALITY OF LIFE?

As we've discussed previously, the point behind the go-for-the-big-potatoes, go-for-the-small-potatoes idea is to pack it all in—to fill your life with valuable contents, the more the better. Dying at 20 deprives you of goods you'd have gotten if you'd lived to 30, and dying at 40 deprives you of goods that would have come to you if only you'd lived to 70 or 80. I think we can generally agree that, all else being equal, the longer your life, the better. No chalkboard filled with high-level Einstein-type math is needed to figure that one out.

~~Einstein calculations~~

But consider this…

2. ASSIGNING POINT VALUES

a. So here's a life, say 50 years long.

50 years

b. And suppose we quantify the quality of this life, say we give
it 100 value points—whatever our units of measurement for
calculating just how good a life is.

   i. 50 years @ 100 points

c. If you had to choose between your life of 50 years at 100
value points, or 50 years at 130 value points, you'd probably
opt for the second life.

   i. 50 years @ 100 points = okay
   ii. 50 years @ 130 points = better = sign me up!

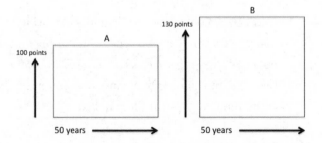

d. Yeah, yeah, quality matters. We know this. But if you think
it through mathematically, maybe it ALL comes down to a
matter of quantity. How so?

3. DERIVING UNITS OF OVERALL QUALITY (sqOQ)

a. When we measure quantity, we need to measure not just the length of the life, but the height of the box: one unit of quality multiplied by each year.

   i. Formula: Duration x Quality = square units of value

Box A = 50 years x 100 value points = 5,000 square units
Box B = 50 years x 130 value points = 6,500 square units

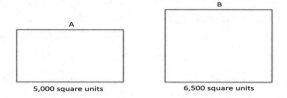

b. Without getting too hung up on the numbers (as though there was any kind of precision here), the underlying principle states:

   i. The area of the box represents "Overall Quality"

      1. —which accounts for the quantity (longevity—how many years you live) and type of items (big and small potatoes—writing *Moby Dick the Sequel: Good Whales Gone Bad* and sipping fine wine) that you managed to cram into your 50-year lifespan box.

c. Now do this: Place each item on either the Big Potatoes or Small Potatoes list.

   i.   Hiking Mount Whitney[6]
   ii. Attending your son's school play
   iii. Gardening
   iv. Watching TV (alone)[7]
   v. Watching TV (with your elderly mother in the nursing home)[8]
   vi. Writing your novel[9]

So then, if…

   i. Potatoes is the same thing as square units of Overall Quality

Then we can say…

   i. Potatoes = sqOQ

Which means…

   i. Potatoes x Duration = square units of Overall Quality
   ii. Formula: Π P x D = sqOQ

Box A = 5,000 square units of Overall Quality @ 50 years = 5,000 sqOQ

Box B = 6,500 square units of Overall Quality @ 50 years = 6,500 sqOQ

---

6. Or the Mexican desert. Or the Amazon jungle.

7. Say a rerun of *Raiders of the Lost Ark*. Or *Charlie's Angels*.

8. *Monk.*

9. *Moby Dick the Sequel: Good Whales Gone Bad.*

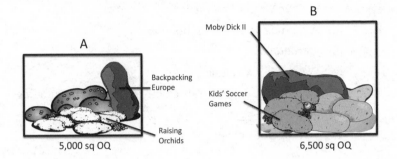

A

Backpacking Europe

Raising Orchids

5,000 sq OQ

B

Moby Dick II

Kids' Soccer Games

6,500 sq OQ

4. MEASURING DIFFERENT KINDS OF LIVES

    a. We could start measuring different kinds of lives.

    b. You could live 100 years at 90 quality points.

    c. Or you could live 150 years at some lesser point value—less quality but longer duration.

        i. We see how it goes:

           Box C = 100 years x 90 value points = 9,000 sqOQ
           Box D = 150 years x 40 value points = 6,000 sqOQ
           Etc., etc., etc. …

5. AVERAGE RANK OF SATISFACTION

a. Now let's compare lives relative to the average rank of satisfaction on the Overall Quality scale. Suppose that…

b. A good life, an average life, ranked at an Overall Quality of <u>10</u>

$$\textbf{10 sqOQ} \approx \textbf{J = good life}$$

c. Zero would be a life not worth having, but no worse than nonexistence (NE)

$$\textbf{0/+1 sqOQ} \approx (\infty\ \textbf{NE}) = \textbf{K = icky life}$$

d. Negative numbers mean you're presumably better off dead (BOD)

$$\textbf{-1 sqOQ} \geq \approx\{\emptyset\} \rightarrow \textbf{BOD = L = TERRIBLE life}$$

e. Comparatively speaking, then, Box A (remember our first box?) is an incredible life after all!

   i. Average life = 10 points of value?
   ii. Box A = 100 points of value?
   iii. Things are looking up.

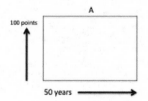

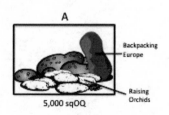

f. Just for laughs, what if we restacked the potatoes in Box A?

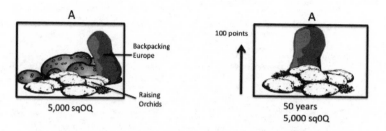

g. Same potatoes, rearranged. Look how much taller! Even better!

6. COMPARING TYPES OF EXISTENCE

    a. Now do this:

    b. First, compare Box A with this very long but unexciting life, Box E

    c. Box E = 30,000 years x 1 value point = 30,000 sqOQ

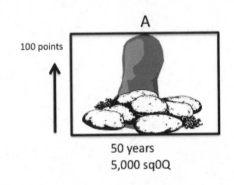

A

100 points

50 years
5,000 sqOQ

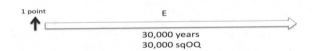

1 point

E

30,000 years
30,000 sqOQ

    d. Next, do this: Choose between these two lives.

        i. Life E or Life A?

    e. Technically, Life E contains more quantity of what matters—

        i. 30,000 versus 5,000

    f. Yet I'm pretty certain most of us would not choose Life E

MID-SUMMATIVE EVALUATION:

Even when we reduce the importance of QUALITY by FOLDING it into QUANTITY, we see that the totals don't account for humanist values.[10]

---

10. Perhaps the authors of the *Choose Your Own Adventure* series were onto something. Taking the canoe is very risky compared to walking along the riverbank, but I'm willing to wager that most kids choose the canoe.

My mother and I, deep in the Amazon Rainforest—we chose the canoe. We knew good and well that the waters were infested with piranhas and caiman and snakes. But we chose the canoe. I'd choose it again.

Hiking with my father through the snake-filled Mexican desert of Cataviña— poking the sand for sidewinders—in search of rumored cave paintings. Worth the risk? It depends on what one values in life. That trip was a do-over for me, a chance to get to know a father I'd not really known until then—a chance to satisfy my curiosity as well as ease my conscience—what if he were to die before I ever got to know him? I preempted future regrets by choosing a new ending to the Estranged Father story. Taking that road trip gave us the occasion to talk, leisurely and in depth, to let the long silences settle around us when we'd tired of conversation, to simply inhale the sun-baked oxygen perfumed with cactus blooms.

7. MEASURING PEAKS

a. What else might we consider when choosing between lives A and E?

b. Even though Life A is shorter, it attains a kind of peak, a kind of...

HEIGHT

c. ...that isn't approached anyplace in Life E.

d. Perhaps, then, in evaluating and choosing between rival lives, we should

CONSIDER THE PEAKS

e. Look at the heights. Think not just about how much you packed in, but determine your greatest goods, what you acquired or accomplished.

CONSIDER YOUR OWN LIFE:
   i.   Do you have 1 or 2 really huge potatoes in the mix?
   ii. Or do you have tons of small potatoes & none big?
   iii. What's your ratio of small to large potatoes?
   iv. How high are your potatoes stacked?

f. Maybe you just have one or two really giant potatoes, ones that trump a heap of small potatoes. Or vice versa. Maybe nothing matters except the peaks.

g. I think this is what the Romantic German poet Friedrich

Hölderlin is getting at in his poem *To the Parcae* (circa 1800).

In ancient Roman religion and myths, the Parcae (noun; plural) were the female personifications of destiny. The poet wrote:

> Grant me but one good summer, you Powerful Ones!
> And but one autumn, ripening for my song,
> So that my heart, fulfilled by sweet play,
> Might the more willingly die, contented.
>
> The soul deprived in life of its godly right
> Won't rest in Orcus, either, not down below,
> Yet if the sacred boon my heart craves
> Should in the future succeed—the poem—
>
> Welcome, then, silence, hail to the world of shades!
> I'll rest content, even if my lyre and play
> Did not conduct me down there; once I
> Lived as the gods live, and more we don't need.

Hölderlin doesn't care about longevity. If he can accomplish something really spectacular, if he can reach great heights—through his poetry in particular—that's enough.

Once he's lived like the gods, he needs no more.

In thinking about what we want to do with our lives, then, we have to address this question of quality versus quantity. Is quality only important insofar as it gets folded into producing greater quantity? Or does quality matter in its own right as something that's worth going for, even when it means a smaller quantity? And if quality does matter, does quantity matter as well? Or is quality all that matters? Is Hölderlin right when he says *once I've lived like the gods, more is not needed?*

I imagine that Hölderlin is thinking about the lasting contribution his poetry might make. There's a sense that if we accomplish something really great, something lasting, we attain a kind of immortality. We live on through our works.

h. Here's a Woody Allen joke:

"I don't want to be immortal through my work;
I want to be immortal through not dying."

i. Yeah, me too. Sign me up.

j. But given our options, maybe we can take some comfort in the possibility of attaining a certain kind of immortality. Semi-immortality or quasi-immortality. Or pseudo-immortality.

8. HOMEWORK ASSIGNMENT, DUE NEXT CLASS

1) Study the potato stacks below. Note their relative peaks and volume.

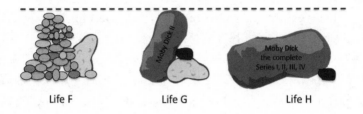

2) Revisit chapter 34 (on creation myths) and chapter 35 (on *Choose Your Own Adventure* books).

3) Read the attached creation myth (a hybrid of sorts), "Cave of Enlightenment."

4) Write your own ending to "Cave of Enlightenment." Be ready to read your story aloud to the class.

Cave of Enlightenment—Part 1

In the beginning there was darkness.

There existed no father-daughter relationship, just two estranged adults linked by DNA and yearly phone calls. Both fear (*What if my father dies and I never get to know him?*) and curiosity (*What's he like? Are we similar? What part of him did my mother fall for back in 1963?*) prompted a circuitous journey, a play-it-by-ear voyage via AAA map, from the Garden of Eden (my cozy apartment) to the dangerous desert of Cataviña.

Father and Daughter wandered through the desert while poking the sand for rattlesnakes, not for forty years, but for at least forty minutes, searching for the makeshift sign pointing the way toward a maze of boulders, a nature-made obstacle course promising enlightenment (in the form of ancient rock paintings) in what they assumed would be a dark cave overhead.

On the trail, Father tromped ahead.

Daughter stepped cautiously, slowly. She stood on one leg for an instant, midstride, listening for the rustle of snakes in the sand, anticipating the moment right before the bite, that sliver of time between question and answer, wonder and revelation. Paralyzed with fear, Daughter weighed the risks—continue or turn back? It was then, in that intermediate moment—the blip of time between the firing of one synapse and the next—that all the worldly knowledge unknown to Daughter, the collective consciousness of humankind, flooded her brain with abstract truth, with the specific answer to the same question, if applied to others—past, present, and future, real and fictional—that would explain her own drive to continue: What if Saint Augustine had not explored his thoughts ("*the disease of curiosity*"), had not written *Confessions*—how would

Western thought have evolved differently had he not taken the risk of applying his background in rhetoric to the principles of Christianity? What if Professor Mackessy at the University of Colorado had given up his research—that risky business of extracting snake venom in plastic measuring cups—which just might lead to a cure for cancer? What if Indiana Jones hadn't overcome, hadn't braved the pit of snakes—how many teenage girls of the 1980s would have missed out on his fictional adventures, the lessons of empowerment and go-get-'em that would someday fuel one of those girls to swim the Amazon River, to live her own real-life adventure, a shared mother-daughter journey worthy of deathbed conversation? What if Daughter and Father turned back now, never made it to the Cave of Enlightenment?

She pressed on.

They made it to the cave.

They sat for a while in the shaded *respaldo* overhang, sipping from their canteens and gazing silently at the primitive, childlike scrawls on the rock wall.

"I have so many things I want to tell you," Father said, "about the origins of life and the universe and what it all means."

That was it, the moment leading up to the cataclysmic epiphany, the pause right before the click.

NOW WRITE YOUR OWN ADVENTURE ENDING

Class dismissed.

PART V

Songbirds

Thirty-Seven

(2005)—

Extending four hundred miles north to south, California's Sierra Nevada mountain range reaches its zenith just a few miles east of our flatland neighborhood in the San Joaquin Valley. From my father's Visalia home just down the street from mine, you can see the rolling yellow foothills of Three Rivers, and beyond, the backcountry's jagged peaks. Early childhood travels with my parents—racing the desert stretches of Death Valley and Mojave and Baja Mexico, inhaling salt-moist winds of the Pacific Ocean, wading the shores of lakes in the Sierra Nevada and San Gabriel Mountains—those early ventures instilled in me a love of nature and travel that has shaped me as an adult, has fueled my wanderlust, my sense of curiosity, and my abiding trust in the raw comforts of the natural world. It seemed fitting, then, to celebrate my father's move from Southern California to Visalia with a trek into nature—just the two of us—father and daughter.

"You *can* name at least one element, can't you?"

This question came from my father, sitting in the passenger seat next to me as we drove the steep mountain highway toward the Sierra Nevada high country, headed for a day hike up Moro Rock in Sequoia National Park. As I drove, my father wanted me to prove I'd been paying attention to our conversation by repeating back to him the list of chemical elements he had just named— the elements that compose the Sun. He wore water-stained, high-top leather hiking boots laced and double knotted just above his ankles, and tucked into his Levis, a faded J.C. Penney T-shirt that bulged at the left breast pocket with a folded white handkerchief. This was supposed to be a celebratory day, but clearly he was on the intellectual clock.

We drove the steep, narrow road that traverses the edge of a mountain high above Kaweah Canyon. Inspired by the beauty of nature as he gazed out the open window—the Kaweah River raging some three thousand feet below us, the snow-covered spires of Alta Peak and Castle Rock piercing the turquoise sky overhead, spent yucca blooms and dried buckeye leaves fluttering at the road's edge—my father had already, inevitably, shifted from general proclamations of awe—"My, how beautiful it all is!"—to scientific and philosophical speculations of ultimate origin—"None of this—the trees, the mountains, the canyon, even *us*—would be possible were it not for the Sun. All life is dependent upon the Sun, you know. *You* would not be possible without the Sun." My father still thrills in his ability to amuse me with his detailed scientific pontifications, most of which I've heard so many times I could recite them word for word—and as usual, I'd egged him on that day. *Yes, I know, Dad, but please continue*, I'd urged him earlier, knowing full well that the trajectory of his current train of thought would first lead to his naming the chemical compounds of the Sun, which would then lead to a lecture on the lifecycle of stars, and would culminate with his favorite trick of all, where he rattles off the entire periodic elements table from memory in under one minute. We were still on step one, though: basic chemical composition of the Sun.

I was negotiating a particularly tight hairpin turn in the road when he asked me to repeat back the elements he'd listed few moments before.

"Well, *can* you?" he asked again.

This is a fun little part of our banter, the part where he quizzes me and I often fail; and in the amount of time I hesitated to respond because my attention was on the road, he spewed his list again, gleefully ticking off each item with his fingers like a schoolboy showing off rote arithmetic facts. "74.9 percent hydrogen, 23.8 percent helium, and about 2 percent metals, which include oxygen, carbon, neon, and iron." He beamed. "Ha! Beat that!"

Thirty-Eight

Perhaps "celebrating" is the wrong word to describe why we drove into the mountains to hike Moro Rock. Moving to Visalia was a transitional time for my father, a bittersweet occasion of uproot. Marina, his wife of thirty-some years, had died a few months prior, and Liza, his twenty-year-old daughter, my half-sister, had died of cancer the year before that. It grew from necessity, then, more than choice, that the old man came to lean on me, his once-estranged, now newly familiar daughter; it was a time to admit his need for someone to look after him, a time to loosen his tight-fisted grip on his own independence.

Not long after he'd settled into his new house, we drove the steep, winding road to Moro Rock in Sequoia National Park. As I recall that day now, two voices compete for attention inside my head. One voice, my father's, expounds the physical characteristics of the Sun—photosphere, diameter, light-years, magnetic fields, ionized iron, solar flares, white dwarf, red giant, black hole—quantifiable facts and theorized algorithms. The other voice, mine, struggles to articulate what the relationship between sunlight and a person might be, and what that relationship might reveal about a particular man standing atop a particular rock in the high Sierra Nevada Mountains; and then, by extension, what does that say about me? What does sunlight reveal in me? What sticks in my mind is the difference in our perceptions that day, my father's and mine, in the ways we each perceived, still perceive, the role of sunlight. What my father sees and what I see are two very different things. With confidence, he identifies indisputable facts. With uncertainty, I intuit shaded variations of humanity.

The sun hung almost straight overhead when we reached the Moro Rock parking area, so we left the car beneath a shady grove of sequoia and ponderosa trees. The rock itself is an exfoliating granite monolith that rises almost seven thousand feet above sea level and protrudes, treeless and sun-baked, over the massive canyon of the Kaweah River, the same river we'd paralleled up the mountain highway. From the trailhead, the hike to the rock's summit is quite short in terms of distance—just a quarter mile—but also rather strenuous, with a three-hundred-foot elevation gain. I followed my father up the rock's trail, basically a series of stairs and ramps either carved directly into the bedrock or formed with massive masonry walls. We stopped several times to catch our breath and take in intermediary views as the path traversed switchback style along the natural crevices and outer ledges of the west face of the rock, but we saved our lingering outward gazes for the dome's top.

I recall so vividly my father's copper hair as we hiked up Moro Rock, a faded hue of the flaming red of his youth, and how it flapped up and down against his forehead when we reached the summit. He leaned against the metal safety rail along the eastern edge, turning his head side to side in order to take in the panoramic view of the Great Western Divide with its striking granite flanks. We stood together in the wind, saying nothing at that moment yet sharing everything in the space and silence of this exposed, barren rock. Far below us, just beneath our hearing, the Marble Fork of the Kaweah raged undetected from our height, the river too distant and masked by terrain to detect with the naked eye. But like the bloodline shared by my father and myself, the river gushed beneath the forest treetops, an artery pulsating through the canyon—fluid composed of hydrogen and oxygen, fluid lit by the sun, capable of supporting life—relentlessly carving itself into the bedrock as if guided by a predetermined DNA map. Like it or not, my father is rooted beneath my skin just as the river flows through the mountain range. We are next-door neighbors, my father and I, partly by default, bound by familial responsibilities and societal expectations, and although he drives me crazy with his certainty, his undisputable facts and well-articulated theories (he is Enlightenment, pure science), he is my spiritual neighbor as well. To experience my father—to spend time with him, peer through the lens through which he views the universe, discover what makes him tick—is to become acquainted with myself. If he is Enlightenment—rational and logical, black and white—then I am Romanticism—experiential and emotional, shades of grey— a difference that vexes me to no end. He responds to nature by explaining the significance of the Sun in terms of a star's physical composition: hydrogen, helium, metals. I noticed something else in that moment we leaned into the guardrail—I noticed the way his body cast a shadow on the rock.

For a moment, my father was not *my* father, but just a man— maybe Old Man Ward Cleaver from the black-and-white sitcom that kept me company when I was a kid, maybe someone else. I saw him as if he were a stranger, or perhaps as he might have ap- peared to any of the European tourists or local day hikers among us. As he steadied himself against the rail, his frail legs now trem- bling from the excursion, his heaving chest deprived of oxygen at such a high altitude—this old man before me, fragile in balance yet remarkably resilient for his age, perhaps like the giant sequoia trees we had passed under—this man cast a shadow onto the rock where he stood, not only with his body, but with his spirit as well. While he verbally expressed awe of the panoramic view, his facial expression, his watery eyes and flinching temple, betrayed a thinly shrouded grief, convoluted as it may have been even to himself. Down around his feet, I saw in my father's shadow the grief he must have felt—for his wife and daughter, both dead so recently; for the career and independence and people he'd left behind in Southern California—a grief he had never articulated to me, not since the move, perhaps not at all.

I suspect this shadow of grief had been following him all day. I imagine it nipped his heels up each of the four hundred or so bed-rock steps and then spread beneath him as he summited the rock; it probably followed him that day as it must have each day: a dark, ill-defined companion that shortens and lengthens with the rise and setting of the sun, that seems to disappear at dusk but reveals itself again each dawn.

If memory serves, as my father turned east, then north, to take in the view, I noticed how the sun had moved slightly in the sky during the time we'd been standing there, and how his shadow had grown a bit longer. It is the angle of light that determines a shadow's length. We can turn from the light and look down, step into its darkness; or face the light and find the bedrock path lit with revelation, follow the illuminated trail, strenuous or otherwise. I suppose we all carry some sort of grief—opportunities missed, friendships lost, attractions forbidden, relationships uninitiated, risks untaken. It's the human condition. Everyone casts a shadow, short at noon, long at four o'clock. Turn your body north or south, yet the shadow always falls opposite the sun—darkness stretches toward more darkness.

I recall the quality of divine, life-giving light as it radiated and diffused around us atop the rock; I recall the way tourists would slowly turn themselves around to marvel at the view, and how most people would pause a moment longer at the view when they were turned away from the sun. We find ways to enlighten our shaded side—equalize light and dark by pivoting toward the sun and then back again, squint in order to accommodate the light's refraction: ah, the flinch at my father's temple, the watery eyes. Or maybe it's the sun that does all the work, and we need only surrender to a certain state of intellectual or emotional transparency. Perhaps if we stay in the light, and if we can manage to preserve our skin from deadly radiation, we will emerge enlightened.

My father and I lingered on the rock for quite a while. We wandered separately—not black-and-white Ward Cleaver and his (unrealized) daughter Betty, but full-color-spectrum Bruce and Carole. We peered over the cliff drop, read the educational signs, got lost in our private thoughts. At some point we asked some-one, a foreign tourist, to snap our photo. Standing over shadows emanating from our feet, we removed our sunglasses and faced the sun so that our expressions would be properly illuminated. In the background of that photo, the Castle Rock spires jut like knives into the sky—dangerous, exciting peaks—and in the foreground, my father's freckled hand rests on mine, both of us grasping the safety rail.

Thirty-Nine

(2006)—

Save for a few boxes in the garage that he never did get around to unpacking, my father had firmly settled into his new house down the street from mine. It didn't take long for me to notice certain things about him. Like how instead of saying hello to the same cashier several times over the course of a few weeks and exchanging ever-increasing bits of small talk—*Nice to see you again. Ready for the weekend? How'd that birthday BBQ for your kid go?*—he'd dive right in with the chemical composition of the Sun, or the dates of Susan B. Anthony's life.

Like the cosmic theory he studies and espouses, my father is a big bang himself. Things happen suddenly. Rather than letting the process of interpersonal relationships build momentum, he goes from zero to a hundred in nothing flat. Whether it's a clerk at the Mexican motel back in 1994 to whom he gives his (and my) entire life story, or the cashier at Save Mart near my home in Visalia, or the woman he currently pines for, he usually skips the normal dance of getting-to-know-you. I often try to control the explosions—either preempt the detonation by neutralizing the social context that's likely to lead to an explosion, or, if that fails, redirect the shrapnel's trajectory—to lessen the damage.

I recall a particular day at the grocery store. "That'll be $15.27," the cashier said.

"Right. Do you take coins?" He pronounced "coins" with two syllables: *coy-ins*.

"Of course."

"Great," he said. He pulled a fistful of Susan B. Anthony dollars from his pants pocket. Slowly he uncurled his fingers to balance the heap of coins in his cupped palm. "I like to use these instead of paper money," he said as he counted them out with meticulous precision. He placed three stacks of silver dollars on the counter, five coins per stack. "These coins have been in circulation since 1979, but most people don't use them as legal tender. I do. I think the problem is that they look similar to quarters, but one can see dollar markings if one pays attention." He held one up and tilted it toward the overhead light so the guy could see the details.

"Yep," the cashier said.

A Muzac version of *Lay, Lady, Lay* played in the background. Grammatically speaking, it should be "Lie, lady, lie." *I will lie down on the bed*, or *You will lay me down on the bed*. I wonder what Ms. Loretta Swift—spinster grammarian extraordinaire—would have said about Bob Dylan's poetic license. (*Now she's cold, dead, and alone.*)

"Susan B. Anthony. She lived from 1820 until 1906," my father said as he placed the last dollar on top of the third stack. He then fished in his other pocket for non-dollar coins. He placed two dimes, one nickel, and two pennies in a straight row next to the three stacks of Susan Bs. "There. Twenty-seven cents. And fifteen dollars."

"As long as it's money," the cashier said with a smile, and swept the coins into his drawer, dropping the dollars into the compartment usually reserved for checks and bills larger than twenties.

The woman in line behind us lifted her groceries and stacked them on the conveyor belt.

"This is my daughter, Carole," my father said to the cashier.

I'd been shopping there for over ten years, so the guy knew me. Not by name, probably, but we'd been exchanging pleasantries for years—the *"Plans for the holidays?"* and *"Hot enough out there for ya?"* sort of stuff. He knew that I wrote travel articles for a glossy magazine, that I usually brought my own cloth shopping bags into the store, that if the fresh blueberries were buy one get one free I'd probably buy the maximum allowed by the per-customer limit, and that I preferred to carry my groceries to my car without the box boy's assistance. I knew the cashier had two kids in elementary school, a fairly new dragon tattoo wrapped around his neck, a wife who worked as an instructional aide, and that he often sat on the bench near the newspaper racks outside when he took a cigarette break. Neither the cashier nor I interrupted my father to say that we were already semi-acquainted. There was no chance, really, because my father went on.

"She once voted for Ross Perot, if you can believe that. Ha ha! But that was a long time ago and I don't hold it against her," he said with a wide-mouthed smile.

And on.

"She's all grown up now, but I'm only seventy-eight—I'm just a spring chicken! Ha! We live on the same street, five doors apart. My son, David, and his family live with me."

And we're off.

The cashier fiddles with his receipt tape as my dad explains the complicated logistics of their collective living situation. He tells the clerk that my brother and his wife are starting a business in Mexico—building a large apartment complex that they will eventually manage—and how for the next few years my brother and his family will be splitting their time between Mexico and Visalia, "living there, here, there," my father says in a singsong tone. He explains that David and Penny stay several months at a time in their Mexico home ("apart, together, apart") while overseeing their Mexico startup business, and how the rest of the time they live with my father in his Visalia home (David and Penny "apart, together, apart"), how my brother will continue with his current California employment until the Mexico upstart business has legs, at which time he will end his California job ("we should all retire at forty") and join his wife and two young daughters in Irapuato permanently ("together at last"). My father explains that he will either precede or follow David to Mexico, and he'll live in my brother's newly developed apartment complex. ("The startup business will then be lucrative. Ha!")

Holy crap.

I was no longer an unknown or loosely associated acquaintance who happened to be accompanying an elderly gentleman to the grocery store. Until then, I could have been a caregiver, a friend, a neighbor. Now we were family. I was fully implicated. In the two or three feet separating me from my father, as we stood alongside the counter with its motionless conveyor belt and its fixed ATM swiper box, an invisible bridge linked the two of us, a double-helix suspension bridge spiraled and anchored hip to hip, father to daughter. I was tethered. If things got out of control, I couldn't simply slip away unnoticed.

You probably think I'm overreacting. You're right. I'm not my father's keeper. And who cares if he's socially awkward? And anyway, my father wasn't the one who felt awkward. He was having a pleasant experience chatting up the tattooed guy behind the register. I was the one having a problem.

The cashier nodded at me. "That's nice," he said to my father.

To others, my father comes across as quirky. Sometimes charming. Perhaps endearing.

"His two daughters, my granddaughters, go to school at Pinkham Elementary," my father said.

I wished I could disappear into the floor. I was thankful that the cashier probably assumed my father's rambling was an old-age thing, which it wasn't. These outings are easier for me now that he's older, because in my mind I can pretend that he's senile, which usually alleviates the burn in my lower chest.

"I moved to Visalia a couple of years ago, shortly after my wife died."

And there you have it—*shortly after my wife died*—he'd just slipped his toes across the tenuous boundary dividing what had been stranger-to-stranger chitchat, from what could have remained an appropriate public exchange to a veiled, albeit probably uncon- scious, slightly inappropriate grasp for deeper engagement. Why must he always do this? He gets people to feel sorry for him—a little at first—and then, if the conversation progresses, like if he's at a restaurant alone, talking to the waitress and the couple at the next table overhears (which they do, because my father talks extra loud now that his hearing's bad), he pours out his life story, which is a story structured to highlight his woes, a story that elicits sym- pathy, even pity, or, on occasion, an anonymously paid tab. *I travel alone because my wife doesn't enjoy travel; I moved because my wife died; I carry a photo of my dead daughter, Liza, would you like to see it?; My only friends live in Michigan and I haven't seen them in twenty years, so I type letters to them on my electric typewriter which I got at Office Depot and I'm here at Kinko's now to make copies of those letters, but you're so kind—What's your name? Charlotte?—you're so kind when I come here to Kinko's, that to be hon- est—and please don't take offence, Charlotte—half the reason I come is to see your bright face each week.*

But why do I care? I wasn't at Kinko's when he poured his heart out each week. I wasn't at the restaurant when the couple at the next table picked up the tab. If I'm not there, it doesn't affect me, right? What was I bracing for, exactly—at that precise moment—there at the Save Mart register? What did I dread?

The cashier's eyes darted to the line forming behind my father. "I'm sorry to hear that. You're lucky to have family here."

Family. You're supposed to look out for your family. Be grateful to have family. Be proud of your family. In some ways I am. As I've said, on one hand, he's a pretty cool dad—adventurous, carefree, inquisitive. Smart. On the other hand, I carry a sense of responsibility so heavy that it strains the double helix bridge suspended between us. Instead of merely noticing (what *I* interpret as) an awkward social interaction between my father and someone else, I actually *feel* it. I *experience* it. I *own* the emotion.

I'm the one doing the overstepping, then, aren't I? I've crossed the tenuous boundary separating my father from myself. How can I not? The line evades me, cloaks itself. Sometimes I don't know where it is, or if it exists at all.

His overextended transparency becomes my overextended transparency. He reveals too much, but I experience the pain on his behalf.

Revealing too much.

I suppose someone could say the same of a writer—of a memoirist or personal essayist. Aren't I doing the same thing here, on the page? Exposing myself? Engaging in a form of public exchange—disclosing intimate details about my life, my past, my thoughts and feelings, my shortcomings, my unfulfilled aspirations—for the purpose of eliciting an exchange of some sort, an intimate transaction between writer and reader?

The difference lies in the fact that when I play the role of discloser, I control the flow of information.

My father controls his flow of information.

When I appropriate the social fallout of my father's flow, when I over-empathize, when I intuit the unspoken responses, the reactions, the judgments of others, I assume responsibility for a combustion of elements over which I have little control. (I suppose, though, in writing this memoir, I've turned the tables. My father has no control.)

"Yes, I'm lucky," he said.

Instead of leaving the bag of groceries on the counter for my father to pick up himself, the cashier lifted it over the counter and placed it in my father's hands. "You have a good day now."

"Right-o." He took his bag and stepped away from the counter, whistling a few notes of Beethoven's Minuet in G. He matched his stride with the rhythm of his notes and veered toward the parking lot.

Forty

Since my earliest childhood, my father and I have veered in and out of each other's lives, at times curving dangerously close. Although we were separated by hundreds of miles and two mountain ranges from the time I was ten until I turned forty, for the first decade of my life we often, albeit sporadically, lived under the same roof. During those early years, I secreted certain objects when he zoomed too far away, and withheld other objects when he veered too near.

From my perspective as a child, our living arrangements seemed unremarkable. I thought nothing of the fact that my dad maintained several simultaneous living spaces for himself. He shared a bedroom with my mother in our house on Ninth Street; he converted the detached garage behind the house into a combination studio-apartment-home-office for himself, which included not only his library and desk but a bed, dresser, and hi-fi record player; and he also bought himself a second home a few miles across town, which we referred to as his "pad" on Magnolia Street. Sometimes Dad lived with us, sometimes at his pad. Some afternoons he napped inside the house, sometimes in his office. Sometimes he brought his visitors into the kitchen for dinner, sometimes they stayed namelessly in the backyard or inside his private office. Sometimes he left for the weekend, sometimes the month. To me, it seemed like an easygoing arrangement between my parents. No drama—not that I was aware of, anyway. I thought all fathers kept separate quarters of some sort and everyone's dad came and went unannounced. While at the time I didn't begrudge him his absences—I didn't know any different—what I wanted more than anything was his undivided attention.

I recall one late afternoon in the living room when he recorded me singing songs as I made them up, impromptu. I must have been quite young, probably about six, a year or so before my brother was born. Our favorite grocery store was going out of business that week, and we had just returned home from our final shopping trip. As my mother unpacked the paper bags in the kitchen, my father suggested I sing a song about Lucky Mart into the reel-to-reel recorder. He held the microphone to my mouth, and as I concluded each song, he clapped, rewound the reels, and played the recording for us to hear. We did it again and again. I made up one Lucky Mart song after another while the world outside our front windows dimmed, until my mother finally announced dinnertime.

Those were the moments I sought.

But they didn't happen nearly as often as I wanted. I suppose that's why I took to snooping early on. When my father was away at work or staying at his Magnolia Street pad, I often snuck into his darkened office while my mother hunched over the rows of tomato plants in the backyard. I secretly pawed through the paper clips and ballpoint pens in the top drawer of his desk, pressed my cheek against the cold cylindrical metal of an unplugged microscope, gazed at—no, studied—the unclothed women in glossy magazines stacked along the bottom bookshelf, slid Jimi Hendrix albums from their jackets to feel the vinyl's grain against my fingertips. Examining and touching these objects brought me closer to the man who owned them. If I couldn't be the center of his attention, then his possessions could, as a convoluted substitute, occupy the center of my attention. I wanted to understand what he liked, even acquire a taste for his proclivities, simply because I wanted him to notice me, to like me. Sometimes I'd put the Jimi Hendrix album on the record player and lower the arm of the needle down. I did not understand this new kind of music, the rhythmless electric grind screeching from the speaker—it sounded like noise to me, like static from an unclear radio station. But perhaps I could learn to like it. So I climbed onto the double bed and bounced trampoline-style while the record spun its noise. I remember watching myself in the mirror that hung on the opposite wall, my bare feet pointed downward in mid-flight, my arms reaching for the ceiling. Jumping over and over, higher and higher, I eventually found the music's beat. Yes, I could learn to like it, even love it. I transformed myself into a living, panting percussion instrument, the soles of my feet plunging into and springing from the mattress—I the drumstick, the bed a drumhead. As my outstretched fingers neared the ceiling, each time with greater upward velocity, I recognized that familiar sensation in my stomach, the same flying sensation I'd felt while riding in the backseat of my parents' convertible when we zoomed full throttle through the California desert.

Forty-One

I recall one summer drive in particular, when I was around five years old. I've already told you how we barreled across the desert toward Death Valley, how gray waves of heat seethed from the highway, how the top of the Karmann Ghia was off and my mother's brown hair flew wildly around her sweating face, how my father stepped on the accelerator and turned up the radio. I sat cross-legged in the backseat with a sweater tied like a turban around my forehead. The empty arms streamed behind me in the wind, rippling between my shoulder blades. I pretended the sweater sleeves were my hair, long and sleek, like the beautiful magazine women my father had thumbtacked to the wall above his desk.

I told you how, there in the car, my mother didn't respond, just stared out the windshield when my father told her a woman would be moving in with us. "Her name is Pat," he said, "and she needs a place to stay for a few weeks."

It was too hot to have anything wrapped around my head, and I imagine my entire body must have been damp with perspiration. I didn't care about the heat, though, and it never occurred to me that I'd be more comfortable without the sweater. Even so, I probably would have kept it on because it made me feel exotic and important.

"Here's the best part of the song," my father shouted into the wind, and he turned up the volume on the radio. I don't remember if he sang the words aloud or not, but I do remember how the road ahead ribboned up and down like a roller coaster, and how I held my breath every few seconds so I could hold onto the falling feeling in my stomach with each decline.

"Faster," I yelled.

Forty-Two

My father has been married six times (twice to my mother). I don't know much about his first wife other than that she was a student of his when he lived in San Francisco, the marriage ended quickly, and I believe there was some sort of trading-grades-for-inappropriate-relations scandal surrounding his termination from that academic post. From there he landed a tenure-track job at Cal Poly Pomona, in Southern California, where he met my mother during her freshman year. They were married from 1963 to 1973, until I was ten and David was three, but it wasn't a traditional setup. Besides my father's numerous living spaces, he often invited students to live with us. I vaguely remember one long-haired couple who kept mostly to themselves, occasionally shuffling glassy-eyed and giggly from behind the closed door of their love den to pour me a bowl of Trix cereal, pat me on the head, and gush at my cuteness—but often the boarders were unattached females my father was either sleeping with or wanted to sleep with.

I'm not sure why my mother went along with this. I attribute her tolerance partly to the 1960s free love culture, and partly to my mother's unusual frame of reference. She'd had a traumatic and unstable childhood. My grandmother committed suicide when my mother was a child. My grandfather, a raging alcoholic and career criminal (among his many schemes: running stolen car parts for the "fence"; moonshine distribution; an elaborate check-cashing fraud), abandoned all four kids in the Ozarks of Arkansas when my mother was ten years old, leaving her to look after her younger siblings, the family living on blocks of government cheese and buckets of water hauled up from the stream. It's nothing short of miraculous that my mother found her way to Cal Poly—a first-generation college student with more family complications than an academic application could possibly reflect. She married my father at eighteen, had me at nineteen. All this is to say: I have a hunch that my mother's unusual upbringing skewed her perception about what a marriage should or could look like.

Although my father was quite busy between his teaching, his secluded study time, and his comings and goings between two houses, he often responded if I asked for his attention outright. I recall one particular Sunday afternoon—I was in first or second grade at the time—when I wanted him to pick me up from home so I could spend the day with him at his Magnolia Street pad. It seemed like it had been quite a while since I'd seen him, several days or maybe weeks. When I complained to my mother that I missed Daddy, she said to call him on the phone and tell him so. I lifted the receiver from its cradle on the kitchen wall and dialed his number. I remember the brightly painted cabinets, yellow and green, and watching my mother wash dishes in the sink. "Busy signal," I said to her. She shrugged. I redialed. Still busy. Again and again I dialed, maybe twenty times over the next three or four hours, and got nothing but a beep-beep-beep. The cuckoo clock above the pantry door had chirped several hourly melodies by the time I got through.

When we got to his pad, I told him about my frustrating day, about how many times I'd gotten a busy signal. "Who were you talking to for so long?" I asked.

"I wasn't talking on the phone. I took the phone off the hook," he said. "Here, let me show you what I was doing."

He went to the bookshelf there in the living room and reached for a large book with a white cover: *The Joy of Sex*. He sat down next to me, cross-legged on the shag carpet, opened the book, and pointed to several of the illustrations—drawings of couples in various lovemaking positions. "This is what grownups like to do," he said, then proceeded to explain what was happening in those pictures and the mechanics of what went where.

When I recount this incident to people now, the story makes them uncomfortable, which in turn makes me uncomfortable. I don't know if that's because my vocalization shades the incident differently for me, like I'm hearing someone else's story, or if I'm reinterpreting my memory based on the facial expression of the person I'm talking to. But while the act of articulating this memory makes me uneasy now, I don't recall such feelings when I sat in my dad's living room that Sunday afternoon. I don't think he meant to be inappropriate with me—I'm not saying he got a charge out of the situation or anything like that—but rather, I believe he meant this as a teachable moment, a time when the topic of sexuality could naturally segue into a conversation with his daughter. An organic birds-and-bees moment.

Or do I protest too much?

Good father or bad?

We had a lot of those moments, times when the double yellow line faded nearly away, blurring the boundary between acceptable cultural norms and inappropriate parenting. The whole question, what's appropriate and what's not, wasn't in his universe.

Around that same time, when my father was staying at our Ninth Street house, I remember joining him in the shower. Some

people might be horrified by a six- or seven-year-old girl showering with her father, but times were different then. Surely other
people who grew up when I did tell stories about their laid-back
hippie parents, about skinny-dipping in a neighbor's pool or growing marijuana plants in the backyard. Perhaps it's a generational
thing. For a certain segment of society, the late sixties and early
seventies culture was considerably lax and earthy and everybody-
runs-around-naked compared to now—at least that's how it was in
my family, or else, how I now choose to contextualize the situation.

As I stepped over the side of the tub and behind the plastic
shower curtain, my father handed me the bar of soap he'd just
lathered up. I held the bar to my nose and inhaled the minty scent
of lavender and hot steam. "Wash everything," my father said as
he rinsed his hair. He gave me an impromptu lesson on hygiene,
telling me how important it was for me to get all the nooks and
crannies of my female anatomy. He wasn't overly explicit, but I
do remember clearly his exact words: "It's important for me that
a woman is clean. I like my women clean, very clean." I lathered,
rinsed, shampooed, rinsed. End of shower, like any other day.

I don't recall feeling uncomfortable that day. But the funny
thing is how vivid the memory is. Like the *Joy of Sex* memory.
Not bad memories, or good memories, but in high-definition
clarity: the silver-framed mirror above the bathroom sink, patterned with droplets of steam; a bar of soap, foamy with the
smell of purple flowers; the living room carpet in my dad's Magnolia Street pad, with its brown specked pattern in floppy strands
of shag. Isolated chunks of tiny details loom disproportionately
large in the landscape of my mind, like pieces of desert gravel
the size of mountains.

Images of certain objects from that time in my life—the mirror,
the carpet strands, the peace-sign necklace hidden in my father's
desk drawer (*Fondly, P.*), the grooves in a Jimi Hendrix album, or

isolated appendages of objects, if not necessarily the articles in whole, like the fuzzy arm of a sweater wrapped around my fore-head—these objects hold so much space in the archive portion of my brain that they push against, almost crowd out my recall of the events themselves. And these objects, none of which I physi-cally possess today, I nonetheless hold dear, keep them clutched in my collection of memories. These objects of my affection are in-animate, objective by their very nature, and they possess no moral ambiguity. A sweater is just a sweater, nothing more. We use it—wear it, wrap it, wash it, toss it. The sweater asks for nothing. Not my affection or my attention. When I—of my own initiation and volition—when I love the sweater, use it, discard it, it truly is an object of my chosen affection. I can objectify the sweater, notice and employ at will. Ah, such power.

I choose to believe that my father had the best of intentions. As with all his other views, when it came to his views on sexu-ality, he was quite forthcoming. Honest to a fault. He shared his views with me all the time, over and over, then as he does now. "Women are baby-making machines," he said to me many times, occasionally as offhanded humorous asides, but usually during one of his talks about sex and where babies come from, and then, later, when he interpreted for me the meaning of the lyrics of "Afternoon Delight." I suppose from an evolutionary stance, he's right. Female scorpions lay eggs, female primates give birth. "Women are," as he's said many times, "baby-making machines." And I suppose that's partly where he was coming from: when this happens, that happens; cause and effect; action and product. Objective observation.

Only once do I remember having a strong reaction during one of our sex talks. I was six or seven years old. My parents had been locked in their bedroom all afternoon. I'd been run-ning around the house nearly naked, wearing only a pair of underpants because it was a warm day, and playing in the front room where natural light beamed through the window. As soon as my mother emerged from their darkened doorway to shuffle toward the kitchen in her robe, I immediately slipped into their bedroom. The pull-down roller shades blotted out all sunlight. "Can I come in?" I asked in the dark. My father said of course I could, but he was going to take a nap. I slid in bed beside him, billowing the thin blue top sheet as I got underneath it, then let it fall down again to drape across my legs. The clink and hiss of my mother making tea in the kitchen punctuated the afternoon heat that seeped in through the edges of the closed window shades.

I don't remember how, but my father quickly segued into another sex lecture, which I listened to with great interest, as usual. It wasn't the setting that made me uncomfortable—not the intimacy of being in bed with my father, both of us in our underwear, or the darkness of the room. And it wasn't the information or the way he conveyed it—holding his fist overhead and explaining that a penis is like a thumb without a bone. These things did not brush against the nap of acceptable father-daughter-ness as I understood it. The information, the digital visual aid, my proximity to my father: so far, so good.

What bothered me were two questions he came around to.

First: "When you're older, say eighteen, will you let a man do those things to you?" he wanted to know. He said that some women are frigid and not interested in sex, and I should not be one of those women. "Will you?" he pressed for an answer.

"I don't know," I said.

He asked several more times, explaining that it's never too early to think about these things, that if I could make him one promise, this would be it.

Each time he repeated the question, I stuck to my answer. "I don't know."

Then he asked the second question: "When you're older, do you think you might pose for *Playboy*?"

Again, I said I didn't know. He repeated the question several times, and I repeated my answer.

Of course I could not have articulated it then, but on some subconscious level I think I understood that if I answered "yes" to either question, I would be making promises I wasn't ready to make and I wasn't sure I wanted to keep. Even in my six- or seven-year-old mind, these promises carried weight, an agreement to carry out specific actions. I might not have had control over who lived in which house, but I had control of my word—to utter, or keep silent. I also understood that my father was not the person I wanted to make those promises to. I already knew so very, very much about his needs and his desires and what he found attractive in women—he'd often pointed out to me what he liked about each one of the centerfolds thumbtacked to the walls in his office. *She has long hair,* he'd say of one photo. *Every man likes long hair.* And then of another photo he'd say, *See how she wears just one piece of draped clothing? That's much more attractive than total nudity. It creates interest, mystery.*

So yes, I knew what he liked—long hair, the fresh scent of lavender, this going into that—and I still wanted to like some of the things he liked, but some part of my child's brain recognized that pieces of a person are not a whole person. If I allowed myself to be bullied into making a promise, I would be giving away an intangible piece of myself. I would objectify my own free will, my autonomy and sense of control; I'd forfeit the sensation of flying I could create at will, depending on how high I trampolined on the bed, how close I got to the ceiling. The prospective acts my father spoke of, the *doing* and the *posing*, those were not what concerned me most, but rather, his request of a promise—that's what violated my senses. Making a commitment that day, that hour, in that room, would have been like slicing my own vocal cords from my throat, cutting loose an utterance that lacks volition when severed from its speaker: a word—a *yes*—that would no longer be my own. I'd be handing something over—like a peace-sign necklace or the arm of a sweater—but that something was an intangible object inside myself: my will.

I don't know how I knew those things, but I swear I did, in my seven-year-old way, and with a certainty that burned through my skin from the inside out. Heat radiated from deep inside my chest, then pulsed through my fingertips and the skin of my cheek and the soles of my bare feet.

And I believe that was the first time I withheld the answer an adult, any adult, expected of me. As we reclined on separate sides of the bed, several times my father again asked, "Will you?" and each time I repeated myself like a scratched record: "I don't know...I don't know...I don't know..." until he rose from the bed in frustration.

"It's hot in here," he said. "I hope your mother is making iced tea."

Forty-Three

Not long after that, my snooping came back to pinch me—not hard enough to make me stop, but enough to make me reevaluate my skills. Along with taking covert inventory of my father's office on a regular basis, I branched into the house. I regularly examined and sometimes played with my mother's stash of Christmas and birthday gifts in the back of the hutch, then acted surprised when I opened my presents. I pilfered from boxes of candy and Pop Tarts stored discreetly on the top shelve of the pantry, then agreed with my mother that yes, we must have a mouse inside the walls.

One particular weekend my father had gone to Hollywood for a night on the town with his friends while my mother, who may have been pregnant with my brother at the time, and I stayed home and watched Peter Falk in an episode of *Columbo*. My father's car sat in the driveway when I awoke early the next morning, so I knew he'd come home during the night. Outside their closed bedroom door, on the cluttered dining-room table, I spotted something new—a 45 rpm record, the same type of black vinyl record as the Hendrix albums in the office, but smaller in diameter, with only one song on each side. I picked it up, held it in both hands, and tipped it from the protective paper jacket. How dare he go out, have fun without me, and bring back this trinket for himself?

I held the record up to the light to examine the spiral grooves. Like I had with the Hendrix albums, I pressed my fingers gently into the surface. First I ran my fingers along the grain, parallel with the circular disc's perimeter; then across the grain, over the grooves from the edge of the disc toward the center. I knew to be careful, because pressing too hard could scratch the groves and ruin the record—the needle would skip when it played, and there's no fixing a scratched record. Where had he gone last night, I wondered. To a movie? To dinner? To the Chinese place with round red doors? And now he had this token.

I pushed my finger harder. I rubbed back and forth across the grain, harder than I ever had with the Hendrix album. And then my finger slipped, and my fingernail gouged a deep rut into the soft plastic. I didn't scratch it on purpose, but then again, he got what he deserved. Maybe next time he'd bring a gift home for me, not for himself. I slid the record back into its jacket and returned it to the table.

Later that morning, as soon as my father appeared from his room, he picked up the record and brought it to me. He held it in front of me, the paper jacket still hiding the scratch. "I got this for you," he said with a smile. "This song reminds me of you. It's called 'I'd Like to Teach the World to Sing.'" He promised that later on we'd go into his office to play it on the hi-fi. "But in the meantime," he said, "it goes like this." Standing between the table and the grate of the floor furnace, with his bare chest and bare feet, he broke into song. "I'd like to build the world a home and furnish it with love, grow apple trees and honeybees and snow-white turtledoves," he sang, then waited for me to repeat the line. Then he sang the next line: "I'd like to teach the world to sing in perfect harmony, I'd like to hold it in my arms and keep it company." He sang the entire song, pausing for me to repeat each line.

He slid the record from the paper sleeve to show me the title printed on the label. That's when he noticed the scratch. "How could that be?" he moaned. "I checked it in the store." He turned the record over and over, examining it closely in the light, then moving to the unshaded window for closer inspection.

I played dumb, never confessing to my little crime. It was an accident, after all. Sort of. And isn't that what I deserved, I thought. Here I'd been jealous of my father's outing, jealous of the thing he'd brought back—a trinket he'd purchased for me.

Forty-Four

My parents divorced at the end of my fourth-grade year, just before my tenth birthday. Not long afterward, my mother moved with my three-year-old brother and me to Visalia, a three-hour drive north from Pomona. For a while, my father made the trek up Highway 99 fairly frequently, staying the weekend every couple of months. He and my mother would hole up in the bedroom during the day, and in the late afternoon he'd saunter from the dim hallway and walk around the house in his underwear before taking us to Yen Ching's for mushu pork with sweet and sour shrimp, where my father, without fail, licked his plate when the waiter wasn't looking, and my mother perpetually scolded, "Bruce, how many times do I have to tell you?"

"What?" He shrugged and winked at me. "Carole, did you see anything? David?"

"No," David said, and we laughed when my mother rolled her eyes.

David and I were always eager to see him those weekends. Between visits I mailed letters frequently, many of which I found in his filing cabinet when I recently cleaned out his house. My father and I share the same birthday, June 2, so a few days before my eleventh birthday, my mother took David and me to J.C. Penney's to pick out shirts we would give him as gifts. I chose a green T-shirt with a photo on the front: a bird resting atop a rusted tin mailbox, the red flag raised. The image seemed to encapsulate my sending those weekly and biweekly letters. When he arrived at our house in Visalia that weekend, David and I ran to greet him in the driveway. He swooped us into his arms and said how much he'd missed us.

As soon as we got inside, I thrust my gift at him, which I had wrapped in plain white paper I'd patched together with Scotch tape and decorated with colored pencils and crayons. I'd wrapped the paper directly around the shirt without putting it in a box, so the asymmetrical package squished and crinkled as I pushed it into his palms.

My mother urged him to wait. "Open it later, Bruce," she said. Her face indicated something I didn't understand at the time.

"No, don't wait," I said. All I wanted was to see the look on his face when he saw that shirt. The songbird, the red flag. How perfect. I would be sure to tell him later on that the bird chirped "I'd Like to Teach the World to Sing."

He sat down on the couch, still holding the canvas overnight satchel he'd brought in from the car. He rested the satchel in his lap and wagged his head side to side, explaining that he didn't have a birthday gift to give me just yet, that he thought we'd all go out to dinner that night to celebrate.

"Certainly you have *something* for her," my mother said. She wasn't asking my father, but telling him. He had something. A thing. Anything. Any object. She stood in the doorway, that liminal space between the kitchen and the living room, as if there was something important that needed to be done at that exact moment, an unspecified task that precluded immediate gift exchanges. It was like she stood in between *here* and *there*, ready to either stand behind me in the living room or call me away to the kitchen, depending on how the conversation between my father and myself unfolded. "You have something, I'm sure," she said again. "Maybe out in the car. Yes, maybe you need to go look for it, Bruce—in the car, under the seats, perhaps—while we stay inside. Carole, can you help me in here?"

I plopped down on the floor across from my father.

My mother stepped back once, no longer in the open doorway, but fully in the kitchen.

My father held the wrapped package in his hands, the paper crumpling between the pressure of his fingers and the soft contents inside.

"Bruce," my mother said, "you told me on the phone before you left this morning that you'd already packed it in the car. Remember?"

Today, I know this was my father's cue. He could have made a big act of searching the car while I watched, all the while muttering under his breath, *Your gift must be here somewhere. Where did it go?*—or else he could have made a covert dash to KMart around the corner while my mother kept me distracted inside the house.

"Oh, yes," he said, and unzipped the satchel. "I do have something. I almost forgot."

My mother then stepped forward, now on our side of the doorway, her hand grasping the frame. I suppose she held onto that liminal position between rooms so that she could call me into the kitchen if my father failed to produce a gift and she needed to distract me from disappointment.

He rooted among his socks and electric shaver, then pulled out a boxed bar of soap. Yardley London English Lavender. It wasn't gift-wrapped, but just in the box it's sold in. "You'll become a young lady soon, so I want you to have this, my favorite kind of soap." I knew this box well. It was the same soap he used all the time—a slightly upper-priced product sold at grocery and drugstores. "Here," he said, and placed it in my open hands.

I fell for it. Wow. What a grownup gift, I thought.

He opened my gift, oohed and aahed over the artistic wrapping paper, then modeled the shirt to show how perfectly it fit.

By the time we left for Yen Ching's, I'd placed my bar of soap, still in its cardboard box, on my dresser, as if it were a delicate porcelain trinket. The soap stayed on my dresser for years. To me, it was a scented decoration. Not a utilitarian bar of ordinary soap, but a solid oval sachet that rattled in my hand each time I shook the box gently from side to side.

PART VI

The Face of Perfection

Forty-Five

(2008)—

Although my father's never been real big into giving gifts to his children or grandchildren for birthdays and holidays, he's quite the gift-giver nonetheless. He might tip a pretty waitress twenty or even a hundred dollars. While visiting his in-laws in Mexico, he might befriend the nineteen-year-old maid (who's married and has two babies) and then, upon his return to the States, periodically mail checks to show his appreciation (along with a standing invitation for her to come visit him in the States anytime, free and gratis). What he really wants, though, is not merely to brighten a stranger's day. He's fishing for a wife. Sometimes the whole business gets a little smelly.

Like with Charlotte.

Charlotte happened a couple of years after my father had moved to my neighborhood in Visalia. He'd been going to Kinko's frequently during the preceding weeks, often daily. I wasn't really aware of these outings, nor did I have reason to care. Although we lived on the same street and we spoke frequently, I was only peripherally involved in most of his day-to-day doings, partly because I wished to avoid the awkward Save Mart cashier and Mexican motel clerk–type situations, and partly because David, Penny, and their two kids lived with him. *Here, there, here; together, apart, together.* I was off the hook.

Apparently, my father had befriended and developed a crush on a married thirty-something clerk at Kinko's while making copies of his correspondence to and from various friends and professional acquaintances. No surprise there. Dad's modus operandi in full force. When he'd gone into the store one afternoon and was told that Charlotte no longer worked there, he begged the Kinko's manager to contact Charlotte and relay the message that she should either call him or drop by his house for a visit. Full knowing that this woman (fifty years his junior) had a strapping husband (with a good job as the manager at Lowe's) and two teenage daughters, my father saw this as an opportunity to woo her, lure her from her husband so she might marry him. I know this sounds improbable, but this is what he does all the time—in his eyes, just because someone is married doesn't mean that person needs to stay married (or faithful) to their spouse. Everyone is fair game. I think this stems partly from his self-centered view of the world and partly from some isolated, out-of-context remnant of the free-love hippie culture of the 1960s. And because my father lacks the social savvy to really sweep a woman off her feet (and because he's most interested in women much younger than himself—a twenty-two-year-old would be ideal), he relies on his generosity to make friends. He's a version of the lonely character you see in the movies, the awkward loner who buys rounds of drinks for everyone seated at the bar. Suddenly, he's everyone's bud, at least until closing time.

The first time Charlotte visited my father's house, he offered cash gifts so that she'd be able to (in his words) "feed her family" during what he presumed to be "a period of financial desperation" for poor, unemployed Charlotte. At first she refused. Then she accepted. Several times, over several visits. Twenty dollars here, fifty dollars there.

It seemed that each of them, the old man and the young woman, had tacitly agreed on their rules of engagement—she allowed him the fantasy of a potential intimate relationship (although during her visits they mostly sat on the couch and talked, as if he were a forgotten nursing home resident and she a candy-striper), and he concluded each visit by insisting she take the crisp bills he fanned from his wallet. I'm not sure which bothered me more: the fact that she took advantage of my dad, or the fact that he painted himself a neglected, lonely old man in need of attention. Taking his money was one thing—her bad, his choice. But the woe-is-me scenario reflected poorly on me—look how the old coot's family ignores him. (Which, of course, my brother and I were trying to do. This is why the whole thing drives me nuts. If I paid more attention to my father, he wouldn't need to buy friends. But he drives me crazy. So I ignore him. I avoid him. And when someone like Charlotte comes around, well—I look bad. And it feels like my father's situation is my fault.)

After a while, David and Penny and I made a point of being at home when Charlotte was scheduled to visit, if for no other reason than to show this woman that my dad was not a neglected shut-in to be pitied but a man surrounded by grown children and grandchildren. Nothing changed. The gifts continued.

When the gift ante reached five hundred dollars a pop, my brother intervened by asking Charlotte to stay away. But instead of going away, she resorted to calling right before coming over, then hanging up if David or I answered. She called daily, several times a day, often into the night. Each time my brother or his wife answered, the line clicked and went silent.

Finally, my sister-in-law took charge. She happened to be there when Charlotte dropped by. At the end of Charlotte's visit, when my father opened his wallet in the driveway, Penny, who is characteristically good-natured, kind, and soft-spoken, followed them outside and stood in the middle of the lawn (behind my father so he couldn't see what she was doing), flipping a double-fisted bird and mouthing, "Fuck you, fucking bitch! Go to fucking hell, you fucking whore," to Charlotte and her teenage daughter as they stood next to the open door of their car. Charlotte blinked her eyes a few times and accepted the cash. She never came back. She now works at Walmart around the corner from us, right next door to the Save Mart where I shop.

Forty-Six

The deal with Sandy Lynn Milmoe started midway through the Charlotte debacle.

"I want to show you something," my father said to me one afternoon. He led me into his living room to show off his latest project, a montage of butterflies tacked to the wall. At Kinko's he'd photocopied and enlarged dozens of butterfly illustrations he'd found in various books and magazines—now cut to shape and Scotch-taped above and all around the mantle. He pointed to some of the smaller images and recited the species names. He swept an open palm near the biggest butterfly of all, an original painting on sixteen-by-twenty-inch art paper.

"I painted that one myself," he said.

The painting looked vaguely familiar. It reminded me of something you'd see in a textbook: detailed and accurately rendered. Unframed, the painting leaned against the wall above the mantle, a thick, heavy-grade piece of art paper propped in place behind the largest of several expensive Wedgwood china bowls and a clear crystal ball the size of a grapefruit.

"*Papilio rutulus*," he said. "Native to North America."

I would later learn that he'd painted the butterfly back in the 1950s, intended as a gift for a student of his while he taught at Stanford during grad school. The girl's name was Sandy. I would also learn that the girl had refused his gift and so it remained in his possession.

It was the montage collection he'd wanted me to see, though, not his painting. Copied cutouts adhered to the wall at various heights and angles. Each butterfly pointed slightly outward from the painting, all headed this way and that, creating the illusion of a herd, perhaps startled, chaotically scattering away from the giant butterfly at center. In the foreground, nestled between Wedgwood bowls, bouquets of red and yellow plastic flowers sprouted from cut-glass vases weighted with light blue marbles.

He waved one arm in a Vanna-like sweep. "It feels like a garden in here," he said.

"Nice," I lied.

He rattled off a few more species names and brief descriptions: *Morpho menelaus* with its iridescent blue wings; *Ornithoptera goliath* with green wings the color of your mother's eyes; *Vanessa cardui*, which is called the Painted Lady. At some point he offered to make additional butterfly copies for me to tape onto my own wall at home, which I politely declined.

I paced the room while marveling at this recreation of the Garden of Eden. Through the open doorway, I noticed a slew of photos spread across his dining-room table. I stepped into the next room to get a better look. Covering the table was an array of identical eight-by-ten black-and-white portraits of a young woman wearing cat-eye glasses and a string of pearls outside her buttoned-up Peter Pan–style collar. Circa 1950. She looked like a young June Cleaver, prim and proper and eager to do all the things June would do, like vacuum in heels while the pot roast bakes and the blue willow china awaits patiently, expectantly, on a starched and ironed tablecloth.

"Who's that?" I asked.

My father explained that these were photocopy enlargements made from a smaller photograph of a girl he'd dated years before he met my mother, back when he'd taught at Stanford. "Sandy Lynn Milmoe," he said. "Milmoe was her maiden name. We've been corresponding."

I'd never heard this Sandy name before, although I've heard the names of many of his past girlfriends—Pat, Rosalie, Fretta, Gerramina, Whoever and What's-Her-Name—those who came before and after my mother, and also those with whom he'd had relationships while married to my mother. Like the elements of the universe viewed through the Hubble Telescope, my father has always bared himself for anyone's observations, with neither hesitation nor reservation. His open-book style, his eagerness to share both the sweet and sordid intricacies of his life—this has led me to believe that from his perspective, his life choices are nothing to be ashamed of, and therefore, within reason. Maintaining extramarital relationships; girlfriends living with us while he was married to my mother; making his wife and baby live in a tent in the back yard; asking his young daughter if she'd ever pose for *Playboy*; pining for and showering gifts on unavailable women—perhaps he hides nothing because in his mind he has nothing to hide, he's done nothing wrong. These rationalizations constantly incubate in the back of *my* mind, not his. They quietly morph, crowd unnoticed, and spread beyond the boundary that separates my sense of agency from my sense of personal responsibility. What to you appears a clear-cut delineation of responsibility—giving money to Charlotte is his own choice—triggers a reflex on my part, a need to fix the problem as I see it, even if my father sees no problem at all.

Who is this Sandy person, and what mess will I need to clean up now?

"Corresponding?" I asked.

He offered to let me read the letters—in fact, he urged me to read them—that day and many times thereafter. He was proud of this connection he'd reestablished.

The phone rang just as he handed me a manila file folder labeled SANDY LYNN MILMOE.

I picked it up. "Hello," I said into the receiver.

Silence. Click. Surely it was Charlotte trying to get through to my father, but I didn't want him to know. Even though I had planned to keep my visit that day very short, I didn't want her keeping my father company, either.

"Who?" I said into the disconnected line. "Jack? No Jack here. You must have the wrong number."

Forty-Seven

The folder contained several letters, both to and from Sandy. And as I read the first letter (which I'll share with you), I crossed the line from rational person to raving lunatic. I'm still trying to figure out why I reacted so strongly. I'm ashamed to admit it now, but I went pretty bonkers.

The first letter, even at a glance, seemed quite long for an initial query meant to reestablish an old acquaintance from fifty years past. The Facebook or email equivalents I've personally sent and received are typically pretty short—*Hey, So-and-so, is this you? Do you remember me? If so, I hope to hear back from you.* Not so with my dad. This letter (typed on a typewriter rather than a computer) ran two pages long, single-spaced with eighth-inch margins.

July 9, 2008
Dear Sandy,
You will remember me as a Stanford acquaintance, laboratory instructor in biology, admirer and confidant. We dated a few times, and I was highly enamored with you. I was delighted when you told me you are Jewish, and responded by telling you that I am half Jewish.

Here we go, I thought to myself. Rushing in with a big bang, zero to a hundred in no time flat, Save Mart style. *Jewish*, three lines in?

> *My dad was Philburn Firstman (1905-1993). He was born in Chicago, and came to California when he was eleven with his parents, who settled in Highland Park, a suburb of LA.*

He'd inserted my grandfather's dates as if he were rattling off the dates of Susan B. Anthony from one of his favorite coins. And just five sentences in, we get a genealogy lesson that links to Judaism.

> *The Firstmans came to the United States in the mid-1880s from Lithuania. Some of them spell their surname Fürstman, and they are all Jews. My great-grandfather, Max Firstman, and his wife, Sarah, were Orthodox. He died in 1939, and Sarah died in 1941. She taught me a few words in Yiddish, which I still remember. I am very proud of my Jewish heritage, so much so that I went to the Jewish Temple on Fairfax, in LA, to take the course of instruction to become converted to Judaism in 1967.*

As I sat on my father's couch reading (in the very spot Charlotte had often occupied), he sat in the wingback chair across the coffee table, watching me.

Contrary to what the letter says, he'd never identified with his Jewish heritage, at least not to my knowledge. The reason he (and my mother) went to temple in 1967 was because he was having an affair with my mother's best friend, Fretta (who lived in the detached granny flat behind our house), who happened to be Jewish. My father dropped out of the classes after a while (after some sort of confrontation between Fretta and my mother), but my mother completed her own conversion. I was raised Jewish as a result—I attended Hebrew school, completed my confirmation in tenth grade, attended synagogue services every Friday night for some twenty years, and even had a full-blown Jewish wedding (the first time around), huppa and all. My father, on the other hand, dropped out of the religion when Fretta moved out of our house. Today, my father could not recite the Sabbath blessing over the wine if his life depended on it. (He often drinks Mogen David, though, which makes him the only person I've met, Jewish or not, who actually consumes it as a cocktail rather than choking down few ceremonial sips.) So why mention his Jewish heritage to this long-lost woman?

"Interesting," I said, hoping he'd stop staring at me.

He offered to turn on the reading lamp, or perhaps I'd like a glass of wine. Or a flashlight? He had plenty of those around, and maybe I'd like one. To see better.

"No," I said, "no flashlight."

You invited me to attend your graduation from Stanford in June of 1959. I couldn't attend because I was embroiled in marrying a student at City College of San Francisco. The marriage didn't work and ended in annulment, but the worst part was that it precluded me from seeing you graduate.

"Embroiled?" I asked.

Thinking I had trouble seeing the text, he jumped up and fumbled for one of several flashlights he kept on top of and underneath the coffee table, which was cluttered with several crystal bowls of hard candy, a box of Kleenex, a half-dozen crumpled tissues, four-by-six-inch glue-top notepads, pencils and pens and *Smithsonian* and *Scientific American* magazines, quite a few DVD boxes, a glass dragon sculpture, and a Native American–style urn filled with artificial flowers.

"No flashlight," I said. "I can read it just fine."

In 1959 you sent me your "goodbye" letter, along with your portrait photo…

Ah, the black-and-white portrait, photocopied and arranged on the dining-room table.

…on the back of which you wrote Gute Glück immer! with your name, Sandy.

"Good luck always"—in German. I would later make the connection that simply because this woman had included a phrase in German, he presumed an explanation—via a huge leap in logic—as to why she ended up marrying someone else. German equals Jewish equals no third or fourth date. In his mind, she had given him a version of the "It's not you, it's me" breakup line.

I was brokenhearted, of course, but I soon realized that your marriage to Gary L. Seaborne was the best thing for your long-term happiness. He gave you more affluence and security than I could possibly have given you at that time. I surmise that Gary was Jewish, and an established widower, with kids, and with property in both Mexico and California (but I'm just guessing).

And if she's Jewish, he reasoned, he would disclose his own Jewishness in this letter as a point of common ground.

I'm also guessing that he was employed with Stanford, either as a teacher, or with SRI. Is Richard Lee Seaborne your son by Gary Seaborne? I assume that by now he is married, and the Internet tells me he lived at various places in Huntington Beach and Foster City. The

Internet also tells me that you lived in various places in Foster City, and that you married Samuel Schulenburg in 1977. He is two years older than you; you were married in Santa Clara, and you just celebrated your 31st anniversary on July 3. Congratulations! I am happy that you are well established.

My dad had recently asked me if I knew how to find people "using the computer" because he wanted to reconnect with an old friend. I'd shuffled him off, lied and said I didn't know how to search names, not because I thought he was up to anything sinister, but partly out of my own laziness and partly because I generally try to keep my interactions with my father as brief as possible—even the simplest interactions with him require a mental complexity on my part that feels like tremendous work. He'd evidently gotten someone to Google this woman's name, though, probably my brother. Or my mother.

But here's the deal: so far, this stuff about why she married this guy, the husband being Jewish and a widower with kids and where he works and them owning property in Mexico...it's pure assumption on his part. With no evidence, he creates these fantasies (here, with Charlotte, with countless others) that account for:

a)   why he's alone
b)   the possibility of his not being alone in the near future.

This happened because of that. Cause and effect. Direct correlation: I'm alone now, these forty years later, because you are Jewish. Ah, that explains it. (She's not, Dad. She's Catholic. But we don't know that yet.)

And what about the word "embroiled" from the previous paragraph? Embroiled? Doesn't this term, in the context of this letter, speak volumes? Might your current use of that word, Daddy dear, shed light on your perpetual loneliness? The state of your current life, your sudden but desperate need to reach out to this woman after all these years? What the hell?

The last time I saw you in person was an accidental encounter at the San Francisco Opera House, where I took my mother to share with me the opera Wozzeck. You sat with friends (or relatives) in the seat row just ahead of ours. I didn't get much out of the opera, but I enjoyed seeing the back of your head during the 2-1/2 hours of the opera.

Stared at the back of her head? Aha! He was crazy then and he's crazy now, I thought. Evidence of his insanity.

In 1974 I think I saw you driving a pickup truck with kids in the back of the truck while I was driving through the city of Cuernavaca, Mexico. I was with my Mexican fiancée. Was that you? All of these years I have wondered. We married in 1976.

I hope this woman's husband isn't a member of the NRA.

I met my dear Mexican wife, Marina (1941-2005),…

Again, the dates.

…through a correspondence club for meeting Latin women.

Marina: mail-order bride number two, after number one—a young, spicy-hot number named Gerramina—didn't work out and fled back to Mexico after six months. He had been engaged to both women at the same time, via correspondence. He went to Mexico to meet them both in person for the first time, decided G was prettier than M—gorgeous, in fact—and called it off with M. G didn't work out, but luckily for my dad, M was still game.

> *She was from the city of Irapuato, in Guanajuato. We were married 29 years before she died. We had a daughter, Liza, who died of cancer in 1999, just nine days before her 21st birthday. Her demise was devastating to me;...*

Demise: one of his oft-used words. Classic. So him. What would I think if I were this woman? What if I were to receive a letter like this out of the blue?

> *...at that time I didn't have faith in personal immortality, as I do now. Modern Null Physics supports the view that we humans are multidimensional, and that there is a dimension of us which is non-physical, and immortal.*

Modern Null Physics. What a comforting thought regarding your dead daughter.

As I read, the phone rang again.

"Hello?" I answered.

Silence, then the faint sound of something ruffling against the receiver on the other end. Click. Charlotte again, no doubt.

"Who?" I said into the disconnected line. "Donald? No Donald here. You must have the wrong number. Uh-huh. You too."

Forty-Eight

My father still watched me, stiff-shouldered in the wingback chair with his hands folded across his stomach, flashlight wedged between his knees should I require more reading light, butterflies tacked to the wall above him.

The letter rambled about what my grandfather did for a living, where the family lived, how many degrees my dad got in college, yadda, yadda, yadda. And then:

> *Sandy, dear, please understand that I am not trying to pry into your personal life. I believe that you made the right marriage decisions, and I respect them. It's just that I love you deeply; forever and beyond forever.*

Not *I've remembered you fondly all these years*, or *I'm writing now because I came across your photo and wondered if you would still remember me.* No. It's a goddamn *I love you fucking deeply, for fucking beyond forever.*

Here we go again, I thought. And we still had Charlotte to deal with.

You see, if this had been a one-time deal, it wouldn't have been be so bad. But my father's behavior ensures that the pattern will repeat. All the time, over and over. If it's not one woman, it's another. And it's constant. Some think he's charmingly dorky. Some get creeped out. Some marry him. Others take advantage of him. I suspect Charlotte started as the former type ("What a charming old man!") then morphed into the latter ("This old fart's practically begging to be ripped off, so why not me?").

Okay, okay. I know I need to calm down. I'm going off the deep end here. I mean, this is textbook Psych 101 stuff, right? Father pushes daughter's buttons (even though he's unaware he's doing so), and daughter totally overreacts. But why does this make me so crazy?

"Maybe you could not stare at me right now," I said to my father across the coffee table.

Don't ask me simply to forget you. I could no more forget you than I could forget myself, or my God. God knows, I have loved you this way for over half a century.

Get ready:

You are more precious to me than the air I breathe. You are more beautiful to me than sunlight on spring greenery; more magnificent than moonlight on the snow-covered Sierras. You are the most beautiful of all possible beautiful women; your precious beating heart is the prime mover of my entire cosmos. You are the epitome of creative perfection.

You see? This is exactly why I get all antsy at Save Mart. At any moment, the counting of Susan B. Anthony coins could change shape, turn into "precious beating heart." Things can get out of hand at any time, any moment.

Next sentence:

Since the beginning of the Big Bang, 13.7 billion years ago, you are the definitive actualization of the goal of cosmic evolutionary history.

Okay. His Big Bang spiel I'd heard a million times.

Yes, there is more cosmic evolutionary history forthcoming. In the end we shall all be sublimely beautiful angels in the presence of God.

But angels in the presence of God? Never.

No one can begin to comprehend how beautiful eternity will be. In our ethereal non-physical bodies we will be able to fly through space faster than the speed of light. We will explore the entire cosmos with its hundreds of billions of stars, and hundreds of billions of galaxies each with hundreds of billions more stars.

He'd cycled through several religions during his life, called himself many things—Jewish, Fundamentalist Christian, Christian Scientist— but for the last thirty years or so, atheist. No angels, no God, no temple, no church, no Santa Claus, no Christmas gifts, no Easter baskets, no Hanukkah dreidels. The first year he lived down the street from me in Visalia, we all bought him Christmas gifts (I gave him a book, Stephen Hawking's *A Brief History of Time*). He didn't give a single gift, not even to his two young granddaughters, with whom he lived in the same house. The second year, he announced at Thanksgiving dinner, "By the way. I'm not buying anyone any gifts this year because I just bought myself fifteen hundred dollars' worth of educational DVDs from The Teaching Company. I'm broke now and I can't afford to buy gifts. So don't get me anything. I don't believe in Christmas anyway."

I can hear the waiter calling me: "Bitter, party of one, your table's ready."

Please tell me where your interests lie…

You never ask about my interests, I thought.

You live in wine country; perhaps you are owners of a winery in Santa Clara County.

A) Delusional speculation.
B) At what point would this woman feel she's being stalked?

How much travel have you done, either with Gary or with Samuel? My travels have been limited to Mexico and Canada.

When my father and I had traveled to Mexico back in 1994, the let's-get-reacquainted road trip to the desert caves of Cataviña, I understood that if we remained estranged, if he were to pass without my knowing him, without my having established new terms of engagement, adult to adult, I would later and forever mourn a missed opportunity. I would always wonder what made him tick. The thing is, though, to understand someone—to know where his interests lie— can be a risky deal. We don't always like what we find. Or you may discover that you are not where his interests lie. Or maybe he's interested, but he doesn't express it in a way you can relate to. Maybe he simply lacks common social skills. Or maybe he's downright self-centered.

But still, oh, so vulnerable, too:

I do a lot of imaginary traveling by watching the Science, National Geographic, and Discovery channels.

As I sat on the sofa reading the letter, part of me felt sorry for him. I thought, Why does he need to reach so far back into his past to this person? Why does he bare his soul like this?

Do you and Samuel and your kids enjoy television? How many languages have you mastered? I know you majored in French. What other languages can you speak? For my part, it's only English and Spanish

with fluency, and with Rosetta Stone, I am trying to master German,
and perhaps Yiddish.

While this letter crosses so many lines of decorum—its inap-
propriateness spans the galaxy—doesn't my father want what all
of us want? To know and be known. And here I am, dissecting my
father's love letter, splaying his words and my reaction for others
to see. What does that say about me? It means I want you—the
reader—to know what I know. I want to be known, too. When
my father asks Sandy, "What other languages do you speak?" I'm
not sure if that's because he's interested in her answer, or if that's
merely a segue for him to share something about himself.

I remember one of the letters I would later find in my father's
office while snooping through his stuff, around the time I stole his
scorpion:

April 4, 1977
Dear Rolf,
...I've been sort of depressed lately because it seems to me that I
haven't accomplished anything important in my career as a professor.
When I was your age I thought that by the time I was my age I would
either be dead or else a world-famous zoologist. Well, I'm 48 and still
alive and nobody.

As I read my father's letter to his friend Rolf now, I'm close
to the same age my father was when he pounded out those words
on his Underwood typewriter. We hope our life adds up to something—has meaning and value. But what satisfaction can we derive
from the mediocre accomplishments—not the big-potato Nobel
Prize accomplishments, but the smaller ones, like mastering Yiddish or German—if we have no one to share our life with, no one
to respond to that German phrase you memorized and rehearsed?

What if your daughter is so weary from the mental acrobatics she performs during her interactions with you that she has no energy to stay and watch National Geographic together?

Sitting in the dim living room with a manila folder in my lap, I wasn't sure if I should be shocked on Sandy's behalf—if I should intervene to lessen the fallout should my father take the letter-writing to the next level (Will she be offended? Scared? Will her children read this and decide to take advantage of the old coot? Will he drive across the state and knock on her door?), or if I should congratulate him for locating an old friend (Perhaps she'll be flattered).

This is why I come unglued at the Save Mart checkout. At the bank. The AT&T store. Marie Callender's. This letter, all that it represents, past and present, bears its full weight upon the double-helix suspension bridge tethering me to my father. The bridge sags, drops to the floor, and buries the line that separates us.

> *My major interests are cosmology and evolution. At Cal Poly University my principal teaching responsibilities were biological evolution (on the sophomore level) and developmental biology (=embryology) for pre-professional students. Evolution and embryology are compatible subjects because they're both about process. For me, Evolution is another word for Creation. Please write to me.*

> *Best regards,*
> *Bruce Firstman*

"You can't send this," I said. "Tell me you haven't mailed it."

"Why not?"

"It's inappropriate." What an insufficient word, *inappropriate*. His lifetime of inappropriate behavior caught up to me at that moment. And here I am, still going apeshit over one more stupid letter, one more stupid assumption, one more breach of social decorum. And because I'm overreacting to my father's eccentricities—I mean really, he's not hurting anyone, and he's not doing anything that bad—I'm the one who looks stark, raving mad. I'm the lunatic. I'm the out-of-control daughter who overanalyzes an old man's heartfelt letter to his long-lost friend. I'm so embarrassed—I know better than to do this. What's wrong with me that my father can still stir up all this drama in my head?

He grunted and smiled through clenched teeth. His head wobbled left to right like one of those cartoonish dolls you adhere to the dashboard with a suction cup.

"It's too much. It sounds creepy. What will her husband think?"

"I don't know why that matters. Here," he said, handing me one of the enlarged photos from Kinko's. "The face of perfection."

Forty-Nine

Later, after calming down, I wondered whether the perfection my father saw in Sandy's image was really a reflection of himself. Perhaps he recognized parts of himself in her photograph, aspects worthy of adoration, worthy of divine inclusion. I suppose he'd fallen in love with the idea of this woman, a smooth countenance untarnished by age and experience and opinions of her own, adoring eyes gazing expectantly into the camera's shutter, eager to know him, appreciate him, understand him. But he never really knew her—so how could he love the person that young woman had become some fifty years later? I suppose my father was lonely, in need of a soul mate, a companion with whom he could share the rest of his days here on earth, and whom he might find again after his death. When he talked in his letter about being "sublimely beautiful angels in the presence of God…able to fly through space faster than the speed of light," I think I understand this version of immortality he yearned for, in spite of the purple prose and dubious theology. Don't we all want to live forever? Don't we hope for something more, something bigger than our earthly selves? Maybe that's why we invent creation stories—if we can figure out where we came from, perhaps we can figure out where we're going. If we once staggered shamefully out of an intelligently designed garden (remember the song my father sang, the record I scratched: *I'd like to build the world a home and furnish it with love, grow apple trees and honey-bees and snow-white turtledoves...*), then maybe there's a chance we'll return again. Or, if we emanated from a cosmic explosion, then perhaps our atoms, once they've dissolved, will crash again, detonate anew, and "fly through space faster than the speed of light."

The face of perfection.

My own petty jealousy crouches inside a tiny box buried in my chest (it sits alongside the ring-sized box of panic from the day I swam the Amazon). It pushes against the lid, threatens to spring forth like a demented jack-in-the-box. Why shower the stranger in this old photograph—and other strangers, too—with unconditional adoration? Why not my mother, when she was your young wife, nineteen years old with a newborn baby, living in a tent in the backyard? Why not your daughter on her eleventh birthday when she handed you a gift, the songbird T-shirt? A bar of soap? Really? I still carry the tune of that certain song in my head: *I'd like to teach the world to sing in perfect harmony, I'd like to hold it in my arms and keep it company.* And I still carry the secret with me, that I was the one who scratched your record the morning after you returned from your night on the town. I rubbed my finger into the record because I didn't know how to express my jealousy, my bitterness over your physical absence the night before, your emotional absence that morning and every preceding day of my life.

How could that be? I checked it in the store.

I don't know.

The face of perfection.

As I sat on the couch across from my father, reading his soul-baring letters to an unearned and unrequited love, the paper butterflies on the wall behind him seemed to swarm around his head, flapping their paper wings like bone-dry laundry broken free from the line, whirling furiously through the desert winds of San Vicente. I recalled the night my father and I watched the meteor shower in the courtyard of the Mexican motel, and how he lectured about the Big Bang and the origins of the universe, how he explained the cosmos in a way that accounted for me, a Carole-centric universe where atoms crash, then dissolve, then reassemble again. The universe, life on Earth—scorpions, butterflies, people—continually shifts from one shape to another, either gradually, like Darwin's theory of adaptation, or suddenly, like Gould's spin on punctuated equilibrium theory. It's the same for relationships between people, too—our connections shift, our circumstances change, our needs evolve—sometimes slowly, sometimes in an instant. But here's the thing: beneath the glow of the meteor shower that night in the desert, my father remained oblivious to the domestic life buzzing around us—men sharing a laugh as they leaned against an open pickup truck, women hanging laundry on the line. In contrast, I was interested in him, and in the children kicking a soccer ball against the courtyard's cinderblock wall, and the fact that I had become a real-life version of the fictional Holly from *Land of the Lost*, living a real-life adventure to recover lost time and familial experiences. Searching for my lost father.

To my dismay, the woman replied to his initial letter and many letters thereafter. They corresponded for several years—I guess *precious beating heart* doesn't bother everyone like it does me. She kept her letters quite brief, rather impersonal, and she specifically told my father several times that she was happily married, did not want to be contacted by phone, and had no interest in meeting up. I don't know if it was on the day my father first showed me the letters or sometime after, but eventually he would show me where he often kept his folder of correspondence and photos: on his pillow at night, so he could imagine her at his side.

The afternoon I sat on my father's couch with the face of perfection in my lap, I didn't know that a few years later he would call me from Mexico to say he'd decided to stay forever. I didn't know he'd say into the phone, "I don't have long for this world. I need you to ship me some things." When he rattled off the list of things he wanted to me to send—his Great Lectures DVD collection from The Teaching Company, his *Encyclopedia Britannica* set, odor-free garlic tablets, and five pairs of leather shoes—he also requested the manila folder containing his correspondence to and from Sandy Lynn Milmoe and the photocopies of her black-and-white portrait. "I have the original photograph here with me," he would say on the phone, "but I need the enlarged copies, too. I don't sleep well here in Mexico. I need you to send me the whole folder."

Fifty

(2013)—

He has the folder.

What he doesn't have is the butterfly painting, the former nucleus of his butterfly montage. I kept it for myself. It hangs on my living room wall now. Not long after he moved to Mexico and asked me to send some of this favorite belongings—not long after I stole the scorpion from his desk and ravaged his filing cabinets— he called again, telling me he had forgotten about a certain painting he'd left at the framing shop, and that I should pick it up for him. The butterfly.

From where I often sit on my favorite corner of the couch, my gaze settles on two paintings that hang alongside each other on my living room wall: the butterfly, painted by my father, and a purple lady, painted by my mother some four decades later, sometime around 1995. The two paintings are diametrically opposed in every way possible: subject, medium, technique, style, and intent.

The butterfly, a meticulously detailed and accurate rendition of a Western Tiger Swallowtail (*Papilio rutulus*) native to North America—including Baja, Mexico, where we frequently traveled as a family during my early childhood, and California's Sierra Nevada Mountains, where my father and I often hiked while he lived in my neighborhood—could pass as a scientific illustration in a biology textbook. The butterfly itself is one-dimensional, void of foreground and background, and there is no use of shading to create depth or perspective. The viewer of the painting peers straight down—through a microscope or magnifying glass, perhaps—onto a specimen long flattened between two glass slides. I wonder how my father achieved such anatomical perfection. I imagine he projected a photograph via slide projector onto the wall, then traced the details onto paper, creating a color-by-number diagram that could be filled in and layered with acrylic paint. I suppose it was a tedious job, one that took him several weeks, perhaps months.

On the contrary, my mother's watercolor painting is a free-form, rather abstract version of my great-grandma Grace, a craggy-faced woman wearing a purple dress and a red hat, her ruby lips pursed at the arch of a permanent scowl. On the realism-abstraction spectrum, I'd say the old woman, while leaning toward abstraction, certainly, sits somewhere near the middle of the continuum. Her jowls protrude at a sharp angle and span wider than her forehead, one shoulder concaves to the armpit, and both arms trail into the ether just above the elbow like a ghost summoning the energy to complete its manifestation. The perspective, though, creates depth: the woman's nose, breasts, right arm, the turn of her head, the angle of her torso. A certain realism in perspective compensates for the watery scrawls, overlapping scribbles, and patchy globs of acrylic.

Their juxtaposition, the butterfly and the purple lady, creates a quiet tension, an unarticulated contrast that holds me captive, taunts me with the promise of some secret, some transcendent truth that, once uncovered, would seem so obvious, so simple.

Dad's painting. Mom's painting. How do I read them, and thus paint myself as daughter? Dad created a perfectly detailed but flat rendition of a non-human organism. He created the center of his montage universe. Mom created an imperfect portrait of the woman who came before us, a rendition that oozes with sharp-tongued personality. I don't know what the paintings reveal. Transcendent truth has yet to whisper in my ear. For now I cling to them both, along with the scorpion.

What I do know: I had such high hopes when my father moved to Visalia. It was an opportunity for a do-over. Come live near me. We'll be one big happy family again after all these years. So what if we'd never been the Cleaver family? It's never too late. You play Ward. I'll play Beaver (or Betty). We'll hike. We'll hang out.

And now here we are, all these years later; our roles, my parents' and mine, have shifted. Like I said—if we had been the Cleaver family, perhaps our new terms of engagement would be simple. Maybe I'd look forward to my daily visit to the rest home, eagerly tuck the blanket around my mother's feet. Maybe I'd urge my father to catch the next flight from Guanajuato to LAX. Maybe I'd stop wondering if I'm a good daughter or bad, if my life adds up to anything yet, and whether or not I'm satisfied with my mix of big and small potatoes.

The answers I seek can't be found in my father's lecture on the origins of the universe. I've long since ransacked his home. I've sent a few of his belongings to his apartment in Mexico. Most of his one hundred and one Office Depot boxes still crowd the shed. I continue to paw through his files of correspondence, analyze his love letters to a woman he'll never meet again, yet to whom he still writes. I'm driven to know my father, understand what makes him tick, what makes me similar to and different from him. Despite my neurotic snooping, I avoid his phone calls and give him all the reasons why now's not a good time to visit.

Like my father, I'm caught in a conundrum of attachment and detachment.

Fifty-One

Cataviña, Mexico (1994)—

When my father and I finally reached the cave, we sat in the shaded *respaldo* overhang. We sipped from our canteens and gazed silently at the mysterious hieroglyphs on the ceiling and walls. Much as we would later on top of Moro Rock, we each wandered in our private thoughts. The rock paintings looked different than I expected. All during the hike I had envisioned we'd find clearly defined symbols—stick figure humans, a blazing fire, rain pelting down from a sheet of clouds, or a mural depicting some adventure, perhaps with a narrative arc. I'm not sure what the pictographs illustrated, with their reddish-brown curves and overlapping lines. In my mind I created a story from the abstract markings, the way you find pictures in a cloudy sky on a hot summer's day or stare at an abstract painting through squinted eyes until a definitive image pops out—that's a sun, a moon, a mountain, he runs toward the cactus, do you see it? One version of the story I reassemble contains seven parts:

I.   Light, Time, and Earth

II.   Scorpions, Snakes

III. Sitting-Up Mud

IV.   Starry Nights

V.   Songbirds

VI.   The Face of Perfection

VII. Presence

That afternoon in the Mexican desert, after we'd stared at the tantalizing rock paintings for some time, my father finally spoke. "I want to talk to you about so many things," he said. "But first, let's take a photo."

Funny thing is, we had forgotten the camera. We hemmed and hawed for a while, deciding whether or not we should go back to the car and get it. I wasn't about to make another round trip through the snake-infested sand—I voted we forgo the photos. My father couldn't be deterred, though. He'd go back for it.

I stayed put while he climbed back down the wall of boulders, down to the trail of deep-shifted sand. I stood at the mouth of the cave for a while, trying to relax in the grey threshold between Snake-Infested Out There and Indecipherable In Here. Today, I wonder which really scared me more—navigating a trail spiked with hidden sidewinders, or decoding a faded story peopled with flawed characters. Out There promises adventure, albeit danger, too. In Here requires a certain kind of attention, where old stories crash, then dissolve, then reform anew, like elements of the cosmos evolving from one life form to the next. Remember Gould: *We originated from an improbable accumulation of accidental contingencies. If the evolutionary tape were played again, there is no way to predict what would happen.*

By now my blip of a lifespan is at least half over. My parents need looking after, and as difficult as our relationships have been,

I cannot turn away, not totally. I can't name the chemical compounds of the Sun or spout the diameter of Saturn, but perhaps I can make a pile of potatoes and see how high they stack up. In the end, I suspect the small spuds will comprise the largest part of my Square Units of Overall Quality. Getting to know my dad—whether or not I like what I find—rates at least medium-sized. Maybe even big. Maybe that's what the universe is all about: finding a neglected part of yourself, a dry and withered row in your personal garden, and nurturing it, growing it, giving it a second chance. A do-over.

PART VII

Presence

Fifty-Two

The sun had shifted farther to the west by the time my father emerged from between two giant stone slabs. He paused at the base of the rock pilings and shouted up to me. From my perch, I watched him climb toward the mouth of the cave with the camera bulging from his breast pocket. Beyond him, the boulders' shadows stretched across the bone-dry terrain. Mirroring the sun's migration, the shadows overlapped, blended together in some places, yet remained distinctly separate in others. They stretched eastward and elongated so slowly that their inch-by-inch evolution was almost imperceptible.

We set the camera on autotimer and posed in front of the paintings. The little red light flashed several times, letting us know when to expect the aperture to open. I reveled in the moment right before the click. *Presence: when time stands independent of past or future; a moment captured on film; an ever-shifting point on the continuum of existence; what liquid prolongs for a pickled scorpion, still moist; where curiosity leads; a grain of sand so fine, so small, it settles, sinks beneath your feet unnoticed, unheard.*

Click.

What next, we wondered. Back to the highway. My father fingered the map poking out of his pocket. "Let's play it by ear," he said.

Acknowledgments

This book could not have been written without the support and guidance of a great many friends, family, colleagues, and editors.

Love and gratitude to my husband, Karl Schoettler, for his support, patience, awesome diagrams, and many (oh, so many) pep talks; and thank you to my family, Bruce Firstman, Aranga Firstman, David and Penny Firstman, Tonya Graham, Stephanie Dethlefs, Peggy Schoettler and the whole Schoettler clan; and to my friends near and far. You cheered me on and celebrated each small step along the way.

I owe a debt of gratitude to all the editors and staff at the magazines where parts of this manuscript were first published as stand-alone essays, with extra special thanks to Stephanie G'Schwind and Karen Tellalian.

I am lucky to have worked with dynamite professors and incredible MFA colleagues at CSU Fresno—a thousand thank-yous to John Hales, who put in an unbelievable amount of work giving me insightful feedback and asking just the right questions (the Socrates of thesis chairing) throughout the drafting process... John, I can't thank you enough; to Steven Church, the best model and advocate a writer and student could have; to my other professors, Bo Wang, Linnea Alexander, Alex Espinoza, and Randa Jarrar;

to Connie Hales and Tim Skeen for coordinating the whole MFA shebang; to all of my workshop colleagues; and for all the brilliant conversations and think-aloud sessions, a heartfelt thanks to my dear friend Liza Butler.

Thanks to many amazing writers who have helped with this book in one way or another—Lee Montgomery, Charles D'Ambrosio, Nick Flynn, David Shields, Brenda Miller, Sara J. Henry, Ashley Wells, Jeffery Gleaves, J. J. Anselmi, Shane Velez, Andrea Mele, Brenda Rankin Venezia, Laura Musselman-Dakin, Yenny Rose, Niki Lassen, Erin Alvarez, Sally Vogl, Phyllis Brotherton, Melanie Weger Kachadoorian, Jackie Heffron Williams, Jamie Barker, Irene Morse, Debby Goehring, Diana Carson, Joni Norby, Nancy Holley, Christopher Scott Wyatt, Erin Lynn Cook, Ethan Chatagnier, Jim Schmidt, Karen Stefano, Ruth Gila Berger, Kimberly Dark, Renée D'Aoust, Jennifer Bowen Hicks, Inara Verzemnieks; and the many good people at CSU Summer Arts, Community of Writers at Squaw Valley, Tin House Writer's Workshop, and Bread Loaf Writers' Conference.

A special shout-out to the entire Dzanc team, especially Michelle Dotter, Guy Intoci, Dawn Raffel, Steven Seighman, Steve Gillis, Dan Wickett, and Michael Seidlinger—thanks for bringing this book to life.

It really does take a village.